Cooking With ETN and Friends

A Collection of Recipes by
Erie Times - News
205 West 12th Street
Erie, PA 16534

A product of type**n**save™ software.

Printed in the U.S.A. by

P.O. Box 2110 · Kearney, NE 68848
800-445-6621 · www.morriscookbooks.com

74987-jm   1

Erie Times·News

Times Publishing Company
205 West 12th Street, Erie, PA 16534
(814) 870-1600 • www.goerie.com

The Erie Times-News is a family-owned newspaper serving the Lake Erie region

Jim Dible, Publisher

Recipe Book Committee Members:
Karen Burchill
Heather Cass
Sheila Coon
Jennie Geisler
Chris Mead
Marnie Mead Oberle
Rhonda Schember
Lisa Shade
Tony Yonko

Project editor:
Marnie Mead Oberle

Cover:
Lamb, prepared by Rhonda Schember
Design, Karen Burchill, CyberInk
Photo, Greg Wohlford, Erie Times-News photographer

ISBN
10-digit   0-9716719-4-X
13-digit   978-0-9716719-4-2

Welcome to Cooking With ETN and Friends, a cookbook for you — and by you. We're pleased so many in our community offered to share their recipes and we think you'll find a more than a few new family favorites in these pages.

Erieites love to eat, drink and be merry (something has to get us through those long, cold winters) and, as with most people throughout the world, food is the centerpiece of our most important life celebrations. From wedding cakes to funeral dinners to baptism brunches to family reunions — wherever two or more are gathered, there is likely to be overflowing bowls of pasta salad, wiggling gelatin molds and bubbling crockpots.

Erie is blessed with a diverse culture whose ethnic recipes have broadened our palate. There are strong German, Russian, Irish, Italian and Polish roots in this community, as evidenced by the many heritage festivals in the Erie area. Newer immigrants have brought Mexican, Vietnamese, African, Middle Eastern and Eastern European flavors to our community.

Erie cooks have a long tradition of preparing their family favorites, many of which have been chronicled in the pages of the Erie Times-News. Food writers Jennie Geisler and Rhonda Schember have picked some of their favorites to be included in this book.

The remainder of the nearly 350 recipes in this book come from you, our readers. When possible, we asked you to include a little note telling us about the recipe. Many credited their mothers and grandmothers. We're pleased you shared these family treasures, and that you included many of your own specialties.

I hope everyone enjoys reading these pages and sampling the many recipes as much as I have.

Marnie Mead Oberle
project editor

Jennie Geisler began writing her Loaves & Dishes column for the Erie Times-News in February 2002 and looks forward to her fifth anniversary in a few months.

Because she has no professional training in the kitchen, she still calls herself a novice, and shares her learning experiences in her weekly column, along with her recipes and nutritional information. She tries to focus on healthy foods and cooking techniques, because, frankly, we all need as much help in that area as we can get.

Jennie lives in Conneaut, Ohio, with her husband, John and son, J.R., who turned 1 in September. Jennie also writes Home & Garden stories every Tuesday.

Home economist Rhonda Schember has been writing her cooking column for more than 22 years. For 21 of those, she wrote with the help of fellow home economist Lynn Clint, who recently returned to Penn State Cooperative Extension, where the two met when their first children were born.

Rhonda, who grew up in North East, now has three adult children, including a daughter, Jamie, 23, and twins Joe and Jody who are 21. She worked for the cooperative extension for 13 years before her children were born and she and Lynn left their full-time jobs.

She's the oldest of six children, and always found a way to help out in the kitchen when she was growing up. Food is in her blood, having learned at the elbows of her Italian mother and grandmother. Her uncles ran an Italian restaurant in Altoona. She cooks Italian food at home, but claims she still can't get her mother's meatballs or her grandmother's gnocchi.

All her siblings love to cook and most live in Erie. They gather with her parents every Sunday to eat Italian food.

Table of Contents

APPETIZERS & BEVERAGES

ARTICHOKE & SPINACH DIP

Barbara Valaitis

4 cloves garlic
1 (10-oz.) pkg. spinach, frozen
  chopped, thawed & drained
1 (14-oz.) can artichoke hearts,
  drained & chopped
1 (10-oz.) jar Alfredo-style pasta
  sauce (I prefer Ragu carb-free
  sauce)

1 cup mozzarella cheese, skim
  milk, shredded
1/3 cup Parmesan cheese, low-fat,
  grated
1 (4-oz.) pkg. cream cheese, fat
  free, softened

Place garlic in a small baking dish. Bake in 350-degree preheated oven 20-30 minutes, until soft. Remove from heat. When cool to touch, squeeze softened garlic from skins. In an 8x8 inch baking dish, spread roasted garlic, spinach, artichoke hearts, Alfredo-style pasta sauce, mozzarella cheese, Parmesan cheese, and cream cheese. Cover and bake in the preheated oven for 30 minutes or until cheeses are melted and bubbly. Serve warm with crackers or small slices of Italian, sourdough bread, or bread chips.

Recipe Note: This is my all-time favorite recipe for dips. It really doesn't take that much time to put together and can be reheated in a microwave. I think you'll enjoy this specialty.

ARTICHOKE DIP

Rose Eller

1/2 cup mayonnaise
1/2 cup sour cream
1 (14-oz.) can artichoke hearts,
  drained

1/3 cup Parmesan cheese
1/8 tsp. hot pepper sauce

Combine and bake at 350 degrees for 1/2 hour.

ASIAN COLESLAW

Jennie Geisler
From the Erie Times–News

1 bag shredded coleslaw mix
4 pcs. center cut bacon
1 medium yellow onion, chopped

1 T. soy sauce
1 T. vinegar

Fry bacon and set aside to cool. Add onion to the fat and brown. Stir in cole slaw mix and allow to steam in the pot until slightly softened. Remove from heat and add soy sauce, vinegar and crumbled bacon. Stir well.

BARB'S FAVORITE HORS D'OEUVRE

Barbara Valaitis

10-12 soft burrito shells
2 (8-oz.) pkgs. cream cheese,
   softened
2 (3-oz.) cans chiles, mild or hot

horseradish to taste (optional)
1 pkg. dried beef, chopped
1 large jar salsa (your preference)

Combine cream cheese, chiles, horseradish and dried beef in a large mixing bowl. Spread onto soft shell. Roll the soft shell, and cut into 1 inch slices. Add toothpicks and dip into salsa. Can refrigerate unused burritos.

Recipe Note: This is a wonderful entertaining dish. I've used this recipe many times for large group get togethers and events at work.

BOURBON SLUSH

Judy Fritz

½ bottle bourbon (fifth)
1 (46-oz.) can unsweetened
   pineapple juice

1 (1-liter) bottle diet ginger ale
1 jar maraschino cherries with
   juice, chopped

Mix all ingredients and place in a large container. Freeze at least 24 hours before serving. To serve, scoop slush into glass at least half full and pour diet ginger ale or diet 7-Up over top and stir.

Recipe Note: A great summer refresher!!

CHAI TEA MIX

Sara Simpson

1 cup nonfat dry milk powder
1 cup powdered non-dairy
   creamer
1 cup French vanilla powdered
   non-dairy creamer
2 cups white sugar
1½ cups unsweetened instant tea

2 tsp. ground ginger
2 tsp. ground cinnamon
1 tsp. ground cloves
1 tsp. ground cardamon
½ tsp. white pepper
1½ tsp. allspice

In a large bowl, combine milk powder, non-dairy creamer, vanilla-flavored creamer, sugar and instant tea. Stir in ginger, cinnamon, cloves and cardamon. In a blender or food processor, blend 1 cup at a time until the mixture is the consistency of fine powder. To serve: Stir 2 heaping tablespoons Chai tea mixture into a mug of hot milk. Yields 36 servings.

Recipe Note: You may choose to omit the French vanilla creamer and use 2 teaspoons vanilla extract instead. To do so, mix the vanilla into the sugar, let it dry, then break the sugar into small lumps. Follow the same procedure as above.

74987-06

CHEESY DEVILED EGGS

Mary Perry

6 hard-boiled eggs, finely chopped
3 bacon strips, cooked and
  crumbled
¼ cup mayonnaise
dash garlic powder

1 tsp. minced onion
½ tsp. salt
¼ tsp. prepared Dijon mustard
1 (4-oz.) cup shredded cheddar
  cheese

In a bowl, combine the first seven ingredients until creamy. Shape into 1-inch balls. Roll in cheese. Cover and refrigerate until serving.

CHICKEN WING DIP

Sherry Rieder

1 large can chicken breast meat,
  rinsed, drained and flaked
1 brick cream cheese

1 cup Frank's Red Hot Sauce
½ cup Ranch dressing
½ cup cheddar cheese

Mix chicken, cream cheese and Frank's Red Hot Sauce in a saucepan. Cook over medium heat until cream cheese is melted. Remove from heat. Stir in Ranch dressing and cheddar cheese. Mix and pour into a pie plate. Bake at 350 degrees for 20 minutes or until it's bubbling. Serve with tortilla chips or celery.

Recipe Note: I like it best warm, not piping hot.

CORN AND BLACK BEAN SALSA

Karen Oliver

1 (15-oz.) can corn, drained
1 (15-oz.) can black beans, rinsed
  and drained
1 med. red onion, finely chopped
1 large tomato, seeded and
  chopped
2 jalapeño peppers, seeded &
  minced

1 to 2 T. minced garlic
salt and pepper, generous
  amounts
¾ cup canola oil
½ cup red wine vinegar
fresh chopped cilantro

Mix all ingredients together. Chill at least 2 hours or overnight. Drain ½ of the vinegar and oil. Add cilantro and serve with grilled chicken, fish or tortilla chips.

CRAB BITES
(Rita's Crab Bites)

Beverly Whiting
Rita Zuber

Erie
Times-News

6 Thomas English muffins, split in half
1 stick butter or margarine

1 (4-oz.) approx. can of crab meat
1 glass jar Kraft Old English cheese spread

Mix margarine or butter, canned crab meat and Old English cheese spread. Spread the mixture on English muffin halves. Bake till crispy at 350 degrees for about 15 minutes. Cut the 12 muffin halves into quarters, and you'll have 48 lovely hors d'oeuvres.

Recipe Note: I don't even like seafood or fish of any kind, but these are dee-lish! Retired Erie Times-News employee Rita Zuber gave me this recipe 20 years ago and it's a keeper!

CRANBERRY CHUTNEY

Jennie Geisler
From the Erie Times-News

1 cup water
1 cup sugar
1 (12-oz.) bag fresh or frozen cranberries
½ cup cider vinegar
½ cup raisins

½ cup peeled, diced apple
¼ tsp. allspice
¼ tsp. ginger
¼ tsp. cinnamon
⅛ tsp. ground cloves

Combine water and sugar and bring to a boil over medium heat. Add rest of the ingredients, return to a boil and simmer 15 minutes. Pour into a medium glass mixing bowl. Place piece of plastic wrap directly on sauce. Cool to room temperature and refrigerate overnight to allow flavors to blend. Bring to room temperature before serving. Makes 2½ cups.

Recipe Note: I can't get enough of this stuff on any holiday. It's great on cream cheese, crackers, turkey, mashed potatoes, and plain out of the bowl with a spoon. Enjoy.

CUCUMBER MOUSSE

Carolyn Schenker

¾ cup boiling water
1 small pkg. lime-flavored gelatin (I use sugar-free)
1 cup cottage cheese
1 cup mayonnaise (I use low-fat)

2 T. grated onion
¾ cup grated cucumber with peel left on (I use gourmet cucumber)
1 cup slivered almonds (optional)

Pour boiling water on gelatin, cool; add cottage cheese, mayo, grated onion, cucumber and nuts. Pour into wet mold and refrigerate.

74987-06

CUCUMBER SPREAD

Melissa Lesniewski

1 (12-oz.) soft -spread cream cheese	⅛ tsp. hot pepper sauce
1 med. English cucumber (seedless)	bread slices
2 T. mayonnaise	butter

Grate cucumber. You can use a food processor to chop (not too fine). Put into a mesh strainer and sprinkle with a little salt. Let drain for at least 1 hour. Squeeze excess water from cucumber. While cucumber is draining, combine the mayonnaise, hot pepper sauce and cream cheese and blend together. Once cucumber is drained well, combine all ingredients, mix well and chill overnight. Spread a thin layer of butter on each slice of bread, then spread the filling. Cut crusts off and then cut into either squares or triangles.

EGGPLANT CAVIAR

Stacy Wing

4 eggplants	¼ cup sugar
10 red bell peppers	1 tsp. cayenne pepper
1 large white or Spanish onion, chopped	2 (6-oz.) cans tomato paste
3 cloves garlic, crushed	¼ cup olive oil
	salt to taste

Roast eggplants and peppers on grill or bake in oven for 1 hour at 400 degrees. Put in sealed container and allow to "sweat." Peel eggplant. Peel and seed peppers. Purée eggplant and peppers in food processor. In a large pot, sauté the onion and garlic in olive oil. Stir in puréed eggplant and peppers, sugar, tomato paste, hot pepper and salt. Cook over medium heat until it bubbles. Stir frequently and allow to bubble for 10 minutes. Cool and let rest in refrigerator for at least a day to allow flavors to meld. Serve with crackers, bread, or toast, as a dip or spread.

Recipe Note: This traditional Russian dish is somewhat labor intensive, but well worth it!

FABULOUS FRIED ONION RINGS

Donna Donahue

1½ cup flour
1½ cup beer (active or flat, cold or room temp)

3 lg. onions, sliced
3 to 4 cups shortening

Combine flour and beer in a large bowl and blend. Cover bowl and allow batter to sit at room temperature for no less than 3 hours. When ready, slice onion. Melt shortening. With tongs, dip a few onion rings into batter. Place in hot shortening. Fry rings, turning once or twice until an even golden color. Drain on paper towels.

Recipe Note: To freeze: Fry rings and drain when cool. Place on jelly-roll pan and freeze. When frozen, place in plastic bags and freezer. Reheat in 400-degree oven for 4-6 minutes.

HANKY PANKY'S

Jade Conners
Judy Fritz – Friend

1 lb. sausage
1 lb. ground beef, brown & drain
1 lb. Velveeta cheese, cubed
1 tsp. Worcestershire sauce

1 tsp. oregano
½ tsp. garlic powder
dash pepper

Mix together. Spread on party bread (rye or pumpernickel). Bake 10 minutes at 400 degrees on cookie sheet. Can be made in advance - freeze after assembled - don't bake - and then pop them out of the freezer and bake as you need/want them.

HOT ARTICHOKE AND BACON SPREAD

Dave Irwin

5 slices bacon
1 cup mayonnaise
¼ tsp. dill weed
2 cloves garlic, minced
½ cup shredded Parmesan cheese

½ cup shredded Monterey Jack cheese
1 can artichoke hearts, drained and chopped

Cook bacon and set aside. Combine mayonnaise, dill weed, and garlic. Mix thoroughly. Add both cheeses and mix again. Crumble bacon into the mixture. Add artichokes and mix thoroughly. Spoon mixture into baking dish and bake at 350 degrees for 30 minutes. Serve with crackers or toasted bread.

74987-06

HOT BEEF DIP

Catherine Lewis

1 (8-oz.) pkg. Philadelphia cream
  cheese, softened
1 (8-oz.) ctn. sour cream
3 T. finely chopped onions

3 T. finely diced green peppers
4 to 5 oz. dried beef (I used
  Hormel)

Cut beef into about ½ inch pieces. Combine cream cheese with sour cream as thoroughly as possible. Add onions and green peppers. (You may use other colors of peppers, or mixed colors to add color to dip) Fold in the chopped dried beef. Bake in 325-degree to 350-degree oven (preheated) for 25-30 minutes. This can be served immediately with veggies, crackers and/or chips.

KID-FRIENDLY PIZZA POTATOES

Judy Lohse

1 pkg. scalloped potatoes
1 (16-oz.) can tomatoes
1½ cup water
¼ tsp. oregano, dried
1 (4-oz.) pkg. sliced pepperoni

1 (4-oz.) pkg. shredded (or sliced)
  mozzarella cheese
½ lb. hot bulk sausage or
  breakfast links, sliced, browned
  and drained

Heat oven to 400 degrees. Put potato slices and packet of seasoned sauce mix into ungreased 2 quart casserole. Heat tomatoes, water and oregano to boiling. Stir into potatoes. Add browned and drained sausage. Arrange pepperoni on top. Sprinkle with cheese. Bake uncovered for 30 to 35 minutes. Makes 8 servings.

LEEK DIP

Judy Fritz

¾ cup chopped leeks (If leeks are
  not in season, use Vidalia
  onions)
1 (8-oz.) pkg. softened cream
  cheese
1 cup mayonnaise

1 T. white vinegar
1 T. granulated sugar
6 oz. chopped bacon
½ tsp. garlic powder
salt and pepper, to taste

In a medium bowl, mix together all ingredients. Refrigerate 2 to 3 hours, until well chilled. Serve with buttery, round crackers. Yields 2½ cups - 20 servings.

Recipe Note: A mild, creamy dip that puts leeks in the spotlight. This recipe is just as good if using Vidalia onions.

LOBSTER AND CRAB STUFFED MUSHROOMS

Ramona Piazza

Erie
Times-News

2 T. butter
2 T. minced celery
1 T. minced onion
1 T. minced red bell pepper
2 lbs. mushrooms
1 cup oyster crackers, crushed
6 oz. cooked lobster meat, chopped
4 oz. cooked crab meat, picked over and shredded
¼ cup shredded white cheddar cheese

1 egg
2 T. water
¼ tsp. Old Bay seasoning
⅛ tsp. garlic powder
⅛ tsp. salt
⅛ tsp. pepper
3 T. olive oil
⅔ cup shredded white cheddar cheese

Melt butter in skillet over medium heat. Add minced celery, onion, and red bell pepper. Cook 2 minutes, until tender, then cool. Remove stems from mushrooms and finely chop ¾ cup of stems. Set mushroom caps aside. In large bowl, combine vegetable mixture, chopped stems, crushed oyster crackers, lobster meat, crab meat, ¼ cup shredded white cheddar cheese, egg, water, Old Bay seasoning, garlic powder, salt and pepper. Grease two large jelly-roll pans. Brush mushroom caps with olive oil, sprinkle with salt, and stuff with lobster-crab mixture. Arrange caps in prepared pans. Top with remaining ⅔ cup shredded white cheddar cheese. Bake 12 minutes until lightly browned. Makes about 50 mushrooms.

MUDDY CHEX

Brenda Patton

9 cup Chex cereal
1 cup chocolate chips
½ stick butter or margarine

½ cup peanut butter
1 tsp. vanilla
1½ cup powdered sugar

In a saucepan, combine chocolate chips, butter, peanut butter and vanilla. Cook over low heat until smooth. Pour over Chex and gently stir until all cereal is covered. Pour into zip-top bag containing powdered sugar. Shake until all cereal is covered. Spread on wax paper and allow to dry.

74987-06

MUSHROOMS WITH GRAPES AND BOURSIN CHEESE

Carolyn Schenker

mushrooms
grapes

Boursin cheese
Parmesan cheese, freshly grated

Remove stems from bite-size white mushrooms. Put a seedless green or red grape in each depression. Take finger-full of Boursin cheese and cover the grape. Dip mushroom in melted butter and then roll in fresh grated Parmesan. Place on baking sheet. Bake at 350 degrees for 15 minutes. Serve warm.

PARTY CHICKEN TARTLETS

Jeremiah Mulson

2 T. butter or margarine
1 cup finely chopped fresh
  mushrooms
¼ cubes finely chopped celery
¼ cup finely chopped onion
2 T. all-purpose flour
1½ cup chopped cooked chicken

6 T. sour cream
½ tsp. garlic salt
1 (10-oz.) pkg. flaky refrigerator
  biscuits (10-12 count)
vegetable cooking spray
1 T. butter or margarine, melted
grated Parmesan cheese

Melt 2 T. butter in large skillet until hot. Add mushrooms, celery and onion; cook and stir 4-5 minutes. Sprinkle with flour; stir in chicken and sour cream. Cook until thoroughly heated. Stir in garlic salt, set aside. Cut each biscuit into quarters; press each piece into miniature muffin tins coated with cooking spray to form tart shell. Brush each piece with melted butter. Bake at 400 degrees for 6 minutes. Remove from oven. Reduce oven temperature to 350 degrees. Fill each tart with 1 tsp. chicken mixture; sprinkle with cheese. Bake 14-15 minutes. Serve immediately. Makes 40-48 appetizers.

Recipe Note: For ease in serving at party time, prepare filling ahead and cook tarts 5 minutes. Fill and bake just before service for best flavor. Can be reheated. Enjoy!

PARTY RYE - BEEF DIP

Nancy Phillips

1 loaf round rye bread
1½ cups sour cream
1½ cups mayonnaise
1 T. minced parsley
1 tsp. minced dry onion

2 tsp. dill weed
1 tsp. beau monde
1 (6-oz.) pkg. dried beef cut into
  small pieces

Cut hole in bread and pull out bread from cavity; break apart into bite dipping-size pieces. Mix ingredients. Fill cavity with dip. For best results make up to 12 hours ahead. Make your own beau monde by combining ⅛ tsp. ground pepper, ½ tsp. garlic salt, ½ tsp. celery salt.

PEPPERED CHEESE

Peggy Paul

2 cups grated Monterey Jack
  cheese
1 (8-oz.) pkg. cream cheese
1 tsp. fines herbs

1 tsp. minced chives
1 tsp. Worcestershire sauce
1 clove garlic, crushed
coarse pepper

Combine everything except pepper. Shape into ball, flatten and roll in coarse pepper. Can be served with bread, crackers, etc.

PERCOLATOR PUNCH

Cindy Hickernell
(from Bev Swanson)

1 (64-oz.) bottle apple juice
1 (64-oz.) bottle cranberry juice
  cocktail

¼ - ½ cup brown sugar
2 - 3 cinnamon sticks, broken up
1 T. whole cloves

Clean well a 30 cup coffee peculator. Pour juices into peculator and put remaining ingredients into basket. Plug in and perk until done.

Note: punch will be VERY HOT. If desired, part of the juice can be saved and added after perking is done, to partially cool it.

Recipe Note: Great for meetings or parties.

PINEAPPLE CHEESEBALL

JoAnne Bruno

1 (6-oz.) pkg. cream cheese
1 (8-oz.) can crushed pineapple
¼ cup minced green peppers
2 T. minced onion

1 T. seasoning salt
1 cup chopped pecans
crackers for serving

Drain pineapple. Mash cream cheese with a fork. Mix all ingredients together except pecans. Roll into a ball and chill for 1 hour. Roll ball in pecans. Serve with crackers.

74987-06

PIZZA PINWHEELS

Marnie Mead Oberle

1 sheet frozen puff pastry, thawed
½ cup mozzarella cheese, grated
24 slices pepperoni
¼ cup pizza sauce
1 egg, beaten

Cut puff pastry in half length-wise. Roll out a bit with a rolling pin so it is smooth. Spread sauce over both, evenly, leaving about 1 inch along one long edge. Brush edge with egg. Top rest of puff pastry with cheese and pepperoni. Starting with side opposite plain border that is brushed with egg, roll up, tightly. Repeat with second. Refrigerate for about 30 minutes to an hour. Place, seam-side down, on baking sheet lined with parchment. Bake at 400 degrees (very important to have oven heated to 400 before these go in) for about 15 minutes, or until golden.

Recipe Note: If you want to jazz these up, substitute Parmesan cheese or Wegmans 4-cheese blend for mozzarella, 4 ounces of prosciutto for pepperoni and honey mustard for pizza sauce.

QUESADILLA WITH BRIE & PAPAYA

Katie Kloecker–Apice
Katie Riley Kloecker
Katie Apice

4 flour tortillas (6 inch)
(8-oz.) double cream Brie cheese (sliced)
(3-oz.) pasilla chile (roasted, peeled, sliced thin)
(4-oz.) papaya (peeled, seeded, diced)
(2-oz.) olive oil

Divide ingredients into fourths. Place olive oil on a warm grill or sauté pan. Place tortilla on top, then cheese, chile and papaya on top. Keep flame low to melt ingredients. After about 2 minutes, fold tortilla over, making sure tortilla is light brown. Serve warm with guacamole on the side.

GUACAMOLE

4 med. avocados (Haas)
½ tsp. kosher salt
½ tsp. fresh ground black pepper
½ cup brown onion (minced finely)
2 serrano chiles (seeded, veined, minced)
1 bunch cilantro (minced)
½ lime (juiced)

Cut up and mash avocados in a large bowl, set aside. Add salt, pepper, onion. Mix. Add chiles and cilantro. Mix Add lime juice. Mix. Garnish with extra lime slices or cilantro.

Recipe Note: To make guacamole last longer, mix in ½ cup sour cream. To make guacamole a little bit richer, add ½ cup feta cheese.

REUBEN DIP

Holly Graves

1 can corned beef
2 (8-oz.) pkgs. cream cheese
1 cup sour cream
1 cup sauerkraut, drained

2 cup grated mozzarella cheese
1 tsp. brown mustard
2 tsp. ketchup
1 T. onion flakes

Erie
Times-News

Mix everything together. Spread it in a 9x13 pan. Bake uncovered at 375 degrees for 40 minutes. Serve with crackers while warm.

SALSA VERDE (GREEN SALSA)

Maggie Wilson

½ lb. small tomatillos
1 slice white onion, about ½ inch
  thick
1 clove garlic
1 to 2 chipotle chiles, canned

1 bunch fresh cilantro, including
  stems
salt to taste
½ to 1 cup chicken broth
1 T. vegetable oil

Remove the husks from the tomatillos, but don't worry about coring them. Place all ingredients into blender or food processor and blend until smooth. Salsa verde is now ready to eat with tortilla chips or vegetables. Cook in a small sauce pan for 10 minutes over medium low to use with eggs, enchiladas or tamales.

Recipe Note: Serrano chiles can be substituted for chipotle chiles. Chipotles provide a smoky taste, while serranos provide heat to the sauce. I learned how to make this recipe at a cooking class in Mexico. My favorite way to eat it is over eggs and tortillas.

SANGRIA

Sara Simpson

1 bottle Spanish red wine
¼ cup brandy
2 T. lemon juice
2 T. orange juice

1½ T. sugar
1 cup club soda
orange slices
maraschino cherries

Mix all ingredients (except orange slices and cherries) in a large pitcher. Stir with wooden spoon until mixed well. Pour into large wine glasses over ice. Garnish with oranges and cherries.

74987-06

SAVORY CRESCENT CHICKEN SQUARES
Jeremiah Mulson

1 (3-oz.) pkg. cream cheese,
  softened
3 T. butter
2 cup cooked chicken, cubed
¼ tsp. salt
⅛ tsp. pepper

2 T. milk
1 T. chopped pimento
1 (8-oz.) can Pillsbury refrigerated
  quick crescent dinner rolls
¾ cup seasoned croutons,
  crushed

Preheat oven to 350 degrees. Blend cream cheese and 2 T. butter until smooth. Add the next 5 ingredients, mix well. Separate crescent dough into 4 rectangles. Firmly press perforations, to seal. Spoon ½ cup chicken mixture into center of each rectangle. Put 4 corners of dough to top center of chicken mixture, twist slightly, and seal edges. Brush top with reserved 1 T. butter and dip in crouton crumbs. Bake on ungreased cookie sheet 20-25 minutes until golden brown.

Recipe Note: Mushroom Sauce - Heat together 1 can mushroom soup, and ½ to 1 cup milk and serve with chicken squares.

SHRIMP MOUSSE SPREAD
Paula Bendure

¼ cup boiling water
¾ cup mayonnaise
1 pkt. unflavored Knox gelatin
1 (10¾-oz.) can tomato soup
1 (8-oz.) pkg. cream cheese

⅓ cup diced green bell pepper
⅓ cup diced celery
⅓ cup diced onion
1 (4-oz.) can drained tiny shrimp

In large sauce pan dissolve gelatin in ¼ cup boiling water. Add tomato soup and bring to a boil. Remove from heat and add cream cheese using a wire whisk to combine. Then add vegetables and shrimp and pour into a mold or bowl coated with vegetable oil or non-stick spray. Serve with assorted crackers.

Recipe Note: Great recipe for small get togethers or holiday appetizers.

SIZZLING SCALLOPS

Mary Ann Yonko

Erie
Times-News

1 1-lb. sea scallops
1/4 cup minced yellow onion
1 cup thinly sliced fresh
  mushrooms
3 T. margarine
1/2 cup dry white wine

1 cup light cream
2 tsp. fresh lemon juice
1/2 cup Parmesan cheese
salt
pepper
1 T. freshly chopped parsley

Cut scallops in half horizontally into 1/4-inch slices. Melt 1 T. of margarine. Add scallops, cook for 2 minutes. Using slotted spoon, remove and set aside. Add remaining 2 T. of margarine to same pan over medium heat. Add onion, sauté for 5 minutes. Raise heat, add mushrooms and sauté until liquid evaporates, about 5 minutes. Add wine and reduce to half. Reduce heat to low, add cream, simmer for 2 to 3 minutes. Add lemon juice, Parmesan, scallops, salt, and pepper. Divide among 4 flameproof crocks place on shallow pan. Put under broiler until golden. Sprinkle with parsley and serve with fresh rolls or French bread.

SMOKED WHITEFISH SPREAD

Irene Wehan

1 (8-oz.) pkg. cream cheese,
  softened
1/2 lb. package smoked whitefish,
  skinned, boned, and flaked

2 T. finely chopped green onion
1 T. chopped fresh dill
1 tsp. lemon juice
1/8 tsp. freshly ground pepper

Mix all ingredients until well blended. Refrigerate. Makes 1 1/2 cups. Serve with favorite crackers.

SPICY CHEX SNACK MIX

Judy Fritz

2 cups Fritos
2 cups Cheese-It snack crackers
2 cups pretzel sticks
2 cups Corn Chex cereal
1 cup sesame sticks
1 cup nuts, any type
1/2 cup butter or margarine,
  melted

1 T. maple syrup
1 1/2 tsp. Worcestershire sauce
3/4 tsp. Cajun seasoning
1/4 tsp. cayenne pepper
1/2 tsp. Frank's Red Hot Sauce

In a large bowl, combine the first 6 ingredients. In a small saucepan, melt butter, syrup, Worcestershire Sauce, Cajun seasoning, cayenne pepper and Frank's Red Hot; pour over snack mixture and toss to coat. Transfer to an ungreased 15x10-inch baking pan. Bake uncovered at 250 degrees for 1 hour, stirring every 15 minutes. Yield: About 10 cups.

Recipe Note: Much better than the original version!

74987-06

TACO PIZZA

Karen Churchill

1 lb. hamburger	2 rounded pizza crusts

Brown hamburger meat, drain grease off. Spread onto pizza crusts.

TOPPINGS

carrots	chopped onion
black olives	mozzarella cheese
mushrooms	pepperoni
green peppers	1 (12-oz.) jar salsa, any variety
chopped bacon	

Add salsa. Toppings can be your choice. Bake 400 degrees for 20 minutes. The last 5 minutes or so, sprinkle on mozzarella cheese. Can use pepperoni too. Serves 6-8. Makes 2.

TOMATO MOZZARELLA

Irene Wehan

¼ cup olive oil	½ tsp. salt
3 T. red wine vinegar	3 tomatoes
⅓ cup fresh basil leaves	½ lb. mozzarella ball

Slice tomatoes and mozzarella. Arrange on plate alternating slices. Mix oil, vinegar, salt and basil leaves. Drizzle on tomato and mozzarella slices. Serves 4.

VEGETABLE "PIZZA"

Marty Merritt

2 tubes crescent rolls (regular or reduced fat)	assorted chopped vegetables - broccoli, carrots, celery, red/ green peppers
½ pkg. dry Hidden Valley Ranch salad dressing mix	cauliflower
½ cup Miracle Whip	
1 (8-oz.) pkg. softened cream cheese (regular, lite, or nonfat)	

Using a 10x15 cookie sheet, unroll crescent rolls, but do not separate, and place on cookie sheet. Press all perforations together. Bake at 350 degrees for 8-10 minutes until golden brown. Cool. Meanwhile, mix softened cream cheese, dry Hidden Valley and Miracle Whip in a bowl. Spread evenly on cooled crust. Top with veggies. Can garnish with parsley or paprika to make it pretty. Cut in squares. Makes 32 - 2x 2½-inch appetizers.

VEGGIE BARS

Betty Smulik

Erie
Times-News

2 pkgs. crescent rolls
2 (8-oz.) pkgs. cream cheese
1 pkg. dry Ranch dressing
1 cup Miracle Whip
¾ cup chopped cauliflower

¾ cup chopped broccoli
¾ cup chopped green onion
¾ cup chopped tomato
¾ cup shredded cheddar cheese

Unroll crescent rolls and lay in jellyroll pan. Bake as directed. Cool 10 minutes. Mix cream cheese, Miracle Whip, and dressing mix together. Spread over baked dough. Sprinkle with finely chopped vegetables and cheddar cheese. Firmly press down. Chill. Cut into 1x2 inch bars.

Recipe Favorites

74987-06

SOUPS & SALADS

ANYTIME SPINACH SALAD

Cindy Hickernell

1 (10-oz.) pkg. frozen chopped
  spinach, thawed and drained
2 hard-cooked eggs, chopped
3 to 5 slices bacon, diced, fried
  and drained
¼ cup scallions or onions, minced

⅓ to ½ cup light mayonnaise
  (more or less as needed)
2 T. red wine vinegar
croutons (as needed)
2 to 3 shakes paprika
salt & pepper to taste

Drain spinach well. Add remaining ingredients and chill. If making day before, don't add croutons until shortly before serving. Garnish with more croutons and/or chopped egg if desired. Sprinkle with paprika.

BANG-UP PIZZA SALAD

Ramona Piazza

10 plum tomatoes, chopped
3 med. green peppers, cut into 1"
  pieces
2 (8-oz.) cup shredded mozzarella
  cheese
1 (3½ oz.) pkg. sliced pepperoni
1 (2½ oz.) can sliced ripe olives,
  drained
¼ cup chopped onion

⅓ cup tomato juice
¼ cup red wine vinegar or cider
  vinegar
¼ cup olive or vegetable oil
1 clove garlic, minced
½ tsp. dried basil
¼ tsp. pepper
¾ cup seasoned salad croutons

In a large bowl, combine tomatoes, green peppers, cheese, pepperoni, olives and onion. In a small bowl, combine the tomato juice, vinegar, oil, garlic, basil and pepper; mix well. Pour over tomato mixture and toss to coat. Cover and refrigerate for several hours. Just before serving; sprinkle with croutons. Yields 12-14 servings.

BEAN WITH HAM SOUP

Rosemary Repko

1 (16-oz.) bag great northern beans
1 ham hock or ham bone
3 stalks celery (chopped)
1 large onions (chopped)
3 carrots (peeled & diced)

1 bay leaf
1 large can tomatoes
2 T. ham-flavored soup base
salt and pepper (to taste)

Rinse and sort beans. Place beans in Dutch oven. Add water to cover beans. Bring to boil then simmer for 1 hour or until beans are soft. Mash softened beans with old-fashioned potato masher just slightly. Add 4 more cups of water and remaining ingredients. Stir well. Simmer 1-2 hours until done. (Soup will thicken as it cools) Generously serves 4.

BEET SALAD

Debra Hull

12 diced beets
1 large diced onion
1 cup sugar
1 cup vinegar

1 cup water
1 tsp. salt
5 hard-boiled eggs, diced
Marzetti slaw dressing

Bring sugar, water, vinegar and salt to a boil. Add to beets to marinate in refrigerator for 1 day. Drain off marinade. Add eggs and onions. Toss with slaw dressing. Serve.

BLACK BEAN AND PUMPKIN SOUP

Melissa Lesniewski

3 (15-19-oz.) cans rinsed & drained
  black beans
1 (14½ - oz.) can drained, chopped
  tomatoes
1 T. butter
2 med. chopped onions
3 cloves minced garlic

⅛ tsp. salt
1 tsp. freshly ground black pepper
4 tsp. cumin
4½ cup fat-free chicken broth
1 (16-oz.) can pumpkin
reduced fat sour cream for
  garnish

In a blender, purée beans and tomatoes in several batches. In a large pan, heat butter on medium. Add onion, garlic, salt, pepper, and cumin; cook 6 minutes or until onion is softened and light brown. Stir in beans and tomato purée. Add broth and pumpkin; mix well. Simmer 30 minutes. Garnish with sour cream. Prep time: 10 minutes. Cooking time: 35 minutes.

Recipe Note: Adapted from Three Rivers Renaissance Cookbook IV; Child Health Association of Sewickley Inc.

74987-06

CAESAR PASTA SALAD

Holly Graves

½ cup mayonnaise
¼ cup grated Parmesan cheese
¼ cup milk
2 T. lemon juice
2 cloves garlic, minced
1 medium head romaine lettuce,
  broken up

½ lb. cooked chicken, shredded
  and cooled
8 oz. pasta twists, cooked and
  cooled

Combine first 5 ingredients. Toss with lettuce, chicken and pasta.

COLD NOODLE SALAD

Donna Strong

1 (16-oz.) bag of coleslaw
2 pkgs. ramen noodles, chicken
  flavor
1 bunch scallions (green onions),
  chopped

1 cup sesame seeds
1 cup sliced almonds

DRESSING

broth packets from ramen
  noodles
1¼ cup vegetable oil

½ cup sugar
⅓ cup white vinegar

Mix all together, except nuts. Add nuts in just prior to serving. Can be seasoned with salt, pepper, and garlic powder if you wish.

CRISP VEGGIE SALAD

Mary Perry

1 head cauliflower
1 head broccoli
1 cup celery, sliced
1 cup carrots, sliced

1 cup fresh or frozen peas
1 onion, sliced
½ lb. bacon, cooked and
  crumbled

DRESSING

¾ cup oil
¼ cubes red wine vinegar
2 tsp. red wine vinegar

2 tsp. sugar
¼ tsp. salt
¼ cup grated Parmesan cheese

Clean and cut cauliflower and broccoli into pieces (may be blanched with carrots if you don't like raw). In a large bowl, combine all vegetables. Cook vinegar, oil, sugar and salt in small saucepan until it comes to a boil. Add to vegetables in bowl and toss with Parmesan cheese. Cover and refrigerate at least one hour before serving. Yield - 10-12 servings.

CROCK POT CHILI

JoAnne Bruno

1 lb. ground chuck
3 cans chili beans
1 large can stewed tomatoes,
  chopped
1 med. onion
1 stalk celery

4 cups tomato juice
½ tsp. garlic salt
½ tsp. salt
½ tsp. black pepper
1 T. chili powder
½ tsp. Tabasco hot sauce

Brown ground chuck and drain. Combine all other ingredients and cooked meat into a crock pot. Mix well. Cover and cook on high for 2 hours. Reduce to low for at least 4 hours, may cook all day if desired.

CRUNCHY PEA SALAD

JoAnne Bruno

1 (10-oz.) bag frozen peas
1 cup diced celery
1 cup chopped cauliflower
¼ cup diced green onion
1 cup chopped cashews
¼ cup crisp, cooked, crumbled
  bacon

½ cup sour cream
1 cup Hidden Valley Ranch salad
  dressing
1 tsp. Dijon mustard
1 clove garlic, minced

Rinse peas in hot water, drain. Combine vegetables, nuts and bacon with sour cream. Mix dressing, mustard and garlic together. Pour over salad mixture. Toss gently. Chill. Serves 4-5.

CURRIED CHICKEN SALAD

Maggie Wilson

2 cup cooked chicken breast,
  shredded or diced
½ to ¾ cup mayonnaise
¼ to ½ tsp. garlic powder
2 tsp. curry powder

1 sm. white onion, chopped
1 celery stalk, chopped
½ to 1 T. fresh cilantro, minced
salt, to taste
black pepper, to taste

Mix all ingredients in medium bowl. Chill for 30 minutes for best flavor. Serve on whole-wheat bread, pita bread, or over green leaf lettuce and tomatoes.

Recipe Note: A 13 oz. can of chunk chicken breast is an easy substitute for the cooked chicken breast. Vary amount of mayonnaise and garlic depending on desired texture and taste.

ENCHILADA PASTA SOUP

Melissa Lesniewski

3 (14½ - oz.) cans fat-free chicken broth
2 (14¾ - oz.) cans cream-style corn
2 (10-oz.) cans enchilada sauce
1 (4½ - oz.) can chopped green chilies
1 (10-12 oz.) can chicken breast, with liquid

5 oz. vermicelli or angel hair pasta, broken into 3 pieces
1½ tsp. cumin
½ tsp. onion powder
½ tsp. dried oregano
1 med. chopped onion for garnish
shredded Colby-Monterey Jack cheese blend for garnish

In a large pot, combine broth, corn, enchilada sauce and chilies; mix well. Bring to a boil over medium-high heat. Add chicken, vermicelli, cumin, onion powder and oregano; mix well. Reduce heat to low; simmer 8 minutes or until vermicelli is tender; stir occasionally. Ladle into bowls and garnish as desired. Makes about 13 cups. Preparation time: 10 minutes.

Recipe Note: Recipe was featured in the Sunday Erie Times-News.

FRESH BROCCOLI SALAD

Rosemary Repko

1 large bunch broccoli flowerets, cut into bite size pieces
1 large red onion, chopped
1 cup raisins

⅓ cup sliced toasted almonds
16-18 pc. bacon, fried crisp & cut
2 cup mayonnaise
2 T. sugar

Mix all ingredients well. Refrigerate for a few hours. Then serve.

Recipe Note: My friend Joyce gave me this recipe.

HEARTY LENTIL SOUP WITH HAM AND POTATOES

Karen Oliver

Erie
Times-News

2 T. extra virgin olive oil
3 shallots, minced
1 med. carrot, peeled and finely chopped
1 med. stalk of celery, finely chopped
½ cup lentils, picked over and rinsed

6 cups chicken stock
½ lb. red potatoes, cut into ½" cubes
1½ cups cubed ham
3 garlic cloves
¼ tsp. salt
½ tsp. pepper
⅓ cup minced fresh parsley

In a soup pot, heat olive oil over medium high heat. Add shallots, carrot and celery and cook until vegetables are softened, about 5 minutes. Stir in lentils and chicken stock and bring to a boil. Reduce heat to low, cover and simmer 10 minutes. Stir in potatoes and ham, cover and simmer until potatoes are soft, about 10 minutes longer. Serve with Parsley Purée: Combine garlic, salt, pepper and parsley in a food processor. Process until puréed. Serve a spoonful on top of soup.

HEAVENLY SALAD

Irene Wehan

1 cup powdered sugar
1 (8-oz.) pkg. cream cheese
1 env. unflavored gelatin
¼ cup cold water
½ cup milk
½ tsp. vanilla

½ cup maraschino cherries, chopped
1 cup crushed pineapple, drained
½ cup walnuts, chopped
4 oz. Cool Whip

Soften cream cheese. Mix gelatin and water. Heat milk to boiling. Add to gelatin mixture. Stir well and set aside. To cream cheese add powdered sugar and vanilla. Cream well. Add cooled gelatin mixture and mix well. Add cherries, pineapple, and nuts. Stir until mixed. Fold in Cool Whip. Pour in a 9x9 pan. Sprinkle grated nuts on top. Refrigerate for an hour.

74987-06

HONEY-BAKED VEGETABLE-PASTA SOUP

Beverly Whiting

2 T. oil
1 lg. onion, diced
5 qts. water
1 Honey-Baked Ham bone
3 carrots, diced
3 stalks celery, diced
3 (16-oz.) cans whole tomatoes, chopped

1 bay leaf
salt & freshly ground black pepper to taste
2 tsp. dried oregano
½ lb. small pasta (like orzo or rosa marina)
2 cups diced raw potato
parsley to taste

Cook onion in oil on very low heat till transparent. Add water, ham bone and other ingredients except pasta, potato and parsley. Bring to boil. Turn down heat to simmer uncovered for 2 hours. Add pasta, potato and parsley and simmer for another ½ hour. Serve and enjoy!

Recipe Note: You can't beat this soup on a cold winter night in Erie! The original recipe came from a Honey-Baked Ham store in Pittsburgh, and I've just added a few special touches of my own. My husband asks me to make it often!

HOT BACON SALAD

Judy Lohse

1 head romaine lettuce
sliced onion, to taste
2 to 3 hard-boiled eggs
8 slices bacon, sautéed, retain some drippings

½ bottle prepared coleslaw dressing

Prepare lettuce and onion for salad. Add chopped hard-boiled eggs. Sauté bacon and break into 1" pieces. Mix salad with coleslaw dressing. Reheat about 4 tablespoons of bacon drippings and add to salad. Toss and serve immediately! Serve with crusty bread.

Recipe Note: Fast and easy! Almost a meal! Serves 4.

ITALIAN PASTA SOUP

Pearl Schwindt

Erie
Times-News

1½ lbs. hot Italian sausage
2 (29-oz.) cans diced tomatoes
1 (26-28 oz.) jar spaghetti sauce
1 small onion, chopped
2 cloves garlic, chopped
2 stalks celery, chopped
1 1-lb. box small pasta

1 tsp. Italian seasoning
chopped parsley
salt
pepper
grated Parmesan cheese
2 qts. water

In large Dutch oven brown sausage, drain. Add onion, garlic, and celery. Cook until tender. Add diced tomatoes, spaghetti sauce and water. Season with salt, pepper, and Italian seasoning. Simmer for 30 minutes. Stir in pasta, simmer until tender. Sprinkle with parsley and Parmesan cheese. Serve hot.

ITALIAN VEGETABLE SOUP

Linda Raun
Taste of the Country Cookbook
Third Edition

1 1-lb. pkg. ground lean beef or
  ground turkey
1 cup onion, diced
1 cup celery, sliced
1 cup carrots, sliced
2 cloves garlic, minced
1 (16-oz.) can tomatoes
1 (15-oz.) can tomato sauce
1 (14-oz.) can red kidney beans,
  undrained
2 (8-oz.) cup water

5 tsp. beef bouillon granules
1 T. parsley flakes
1 tsp. salt
½ tsp. oregano
½ tsp. sweet basil
¼ tsp. black pepper
2 cups cabbage, shredded
1 (10¾ oz.) pkg. green beans,
  French cut, frozen
½ cup elbow macaroni, uncooked
Parmesan cheese

Brown beef or turkey in heavy kettle, drain off fat. Add all ingredients except the cabbage (I use packaged coleslaw mix), green beans, and macaroni. Bring to a boil. Lower heat; cover and simmer 20 minutes. Add the cabbage, green beans and macaroni and simmer until the vegetables are tender. This makes a thick soup which may be thinned to your taste by simply adding more water. If desired, sprinkle Parmesan cheese on top before serving. Recipe makes 12 hearty servings

Recipe Note: Don't let the long list of ingredients fool you. This soup is quick and easy to make. It's like vegetable chili and it's healthy, too! Per serving: 152 calories; 776 mg sodium; 34 mg cholesterol; 17 gm carbohydrates; 12 gm protein, 4 gm fat Diabetic exchanges: 1 protein; 1 bread

74987-06

LEMON SALAD

Debra Hull

2 small boxes lemon Jell-O
2 cups boiling water
³/₄ cup sugar
2 pkgs. cream cheese

1 can crushed pineapple
½ cup maraschino cherries
½ cup chopped nuts
1 cup marshmallows

Combine Jell-O, water, sugar, and cream cheese stirring slowly to dissolve sugar and cheese. Add can of pineapple then let partially set up. Then add cherries, nuts and marshmallows and let set. Serve.

LIVER GLAZE SOUP

Irene Wehan

2 beef shanks and one soup bone
1 onion
2 sliced carrots
2 stalks celery
1 beef bouillon
salt
pepper
1 lb. liver

1 cup dry bread crumbs
1 egg
1 T. parsley
½ tsp. nutmeg
½ tsp. salt
pinch baking powder
½ cup flour

Combine first seven ingredients in a soup pot with 3 quarts of water. Cook until meat is tender. Grind liver, bread crumbs, and onion until smooth. Combine with rest of ingredients. Add enough flour to thicken. Drop by teaspoon fulls into hot broth.

MANDARIN SALAD

Sandy Reid

Erie
Times-News

DRESSING

½ tsp. salt
dash fresh ground pepper
2 T. sugar
2 T. vinegar

¼ cup salad oil
dash hot pepper sauce
1 tsp. snipped fresh parsley

Shake dressing ingredients in a tightly sealed container.

SALAD

¼ cup slivered almonds
4 tsp. sugar
2 green onions with tops, thinly
  sliced
¼ head romaine lettuce

¼ head iceberg lettuce
1 cup chopped celery
1 (11-oz.) can mandarin orange
  segments, drained

Toast almonds and sugar in a fry pan over low heat stirring constantly until sugar is melted and the almonds are coated. When almonds are golden with the melted sugar, spread out on a piece of foil to cool. Break apart and store at room temperature in an air-tight container. Tear lettuce and romaine into bite-size pieces, about 4 cups. Five minutes before serving, place greens in a large bowl; add orange segments, celery, onions and dressing to taste. Stir to evenly distribute ingredients. Sprinkle with sugared almonds.

Recipe Note: This salad goes very well with the Oriental Cornish hens.

74987-06

MARINATED SHRIMP AND AVOCADO SALAD

Susie Scott

2 lb. shrimp, peeled, cooked, deveined
2 avocados, cut into bite-sized pieces

12 mushrooms, sliced
2 small onions, sliced

Combine the shrimp, onions and mushrooms in a bowl; toss lightly. Pour in the lemon thyme marinade and toss gently to coat. Chill, covered in the refrigerator for 12-24 hours. Add avocados 2 hours before serving. DRAIN marinade before serving.

LEMON THYME MARINADE

1 cup white wine vinegar
½ cup water
½ cup lemon juice
1 cup vegetable oil
1 T. salt

¼ tsp. pepper
1 tsp. dried thyme
1 tsp. dried oregano
1 tsp. prepared mustard
2 T. sugar

Combine white wine vinegar, water, lemon juice, oil, salt, pepper, thyme, oregano, sugar, and mustard in a medium bowl until well combined.

Recipe Note: Great recipe for a buffet!

MOM'S BEST VEGETABLE SOUP

Sandy Reid

1 large pkg. Sam's Club short ribs, 8 in a pack
1 bag frozen mixed vegetables
2 bags baby fordhook lima beans
1 large can crushed tomatoes with juice
1 to 2 cups chunked potatoes (optional)

1 large Vidalia or OSO onion, chunky chopped
3 T. butter
3 heaping T. beef bouillon paste softened with water
1 pkg. hearty soup noodles

This is best to do over a cold winter weekend. Take short ribs and place on a sheet or oblong casserole pan and bake at 350 degrees for about 90 minutes. Place the roasted short ribs and pan drippings in a large stock pot with just enough water to cover. Simmer for about an hour. Allow broth with meat to cool in the refrigerator and remove the fat that has hardened on top. Remove the hardened fat from the top of the broth and meat from the bone. Chop meat into bite-sized pieces and return to broth. Add veggies, salt and pepper to taste. Melt the butter in a small sauce pan and add chopped onions and cook until soft and translucent. Add to soup. Soften beef bouillon paste with warm water and add to pot. Cook some hearty noodles as directed. Drain.

NUTTY BROCCOLI SLAW

Caroline Mulson

1 (3-oz.) pkg. chicken ramen
noodles
1 (16-oz.) pkg. broccoli slaw mix
2 cups sliced green onions (about
2 bunches)
1½ cups broccoli florets
1 (6-oz.) can ripe black olives,
drained and halved

1 cup sunflower kernels, toasted
½ cup slivered almonds, toasted
½ cup sugar
½ cup cider vinegar
½ cup olive oil

Set aside the noodle seasoning packet; crush the noodles and place in a large bowl. Add the slaw mix, onions, broccoli, olives, sunflower kernels and almonds. In a jar with a tight-fitting lid, combine the sugar vinegar, oil and contents of the seasoning packet; shake well. Drizzle over salad and toss to coat. Serve immediately.

Recipe Note: Yield: 16 servings

PINEAPPLE GELATIN SALAD

Arlene Spaulding

1 (20-oz.) can crushed pineapple
1 (8-oz.) pkg. cream cheese,
softened
1 (12-oz.) carton frozen whipped
topping, thawed

¾ cup sugar
3 T. lemon juice
3 T. water
2 T. all-purpose flour
2 egg yolks, lightly beaten

Drain pineapple, reserving juice. Dissolve gelatin in water. Add pineapple. Pour into an 9x13x2 inch dish. Chill until almost set, about 45 minutes. In a mixing bowl beat cream cheese and whipped topping until smooth. Carefully spread over gelatin and chill for 30 minutes. Meanwhile, in a saucepan over medium heat combine sugar, lemon juice, water, flour, egg yolks and reserved pineapple juice. Bring to a boil, stirring constantly. Cook 1 minute or until thick. Cool. Carefully spread over cream cheese layer. Chill for 1 hour. Serve.

PINK SUMMER SALAD

Nancy Holcomb

1 can cherry pie filling
1 similar-sized can crushed
pineapple, drained well
1 can sweetened condensed milk

1 12-oz. container whipped topping
¼ c. finely chopped walnuts, if
desired

Place whipped topping in large bowl. Add all ingredients and fold gently until mixed well. Refrigerate.

Recipe Note: Cool, quick, easy, delicious.

74987-06

POTATO SALAD

Rose Moorhead

8 med. red potatoes
6 green onions
6 hard-cooked eggs

1 cup sour cream
2 cups mayonnaise
1 env. Ranch dressing mix

Cook potatoes, cool, leave skin on. Cut potatoes. Add finely chopped onions and eggs. Sprinkle with envelope of dry Ranch dressing mix. Mix sour cream and mayonnaise with wire whisk. Blend into potato mixture. Refrigerate for several hours or overnight.

PRETZEL SALAD

Betty Smulik

2 cups crushed pretzels
¾ cup melted margarine
3 T. sugar
1 cup sugar

1 (8-oz.) pkg. cream cheese
2 cups Cool Whip
2 small boxes strawberry Jell-O
2 (10-oz.) approx. strawberries

Mix together first 3 ingredients. Next beat together 1 cup of sugar and cream cheese. Fold in the Cool Whip. Mix 2 small boxes of strawberry Jell-O in 2 cups of boiling water until dissolved. Add strawberries. Stir until thickened. Pour over creamed mix that has been spread over crust. Top with Cool Whip. Store in refrigerator.

SAUSAGE POTATO SOUP

Mary Perry

1 lb. Italian sausage (hot or sweet)
1 cup sliced celery
½ cup chopped onion
½ tsp. dried thyme
2 T. all-purpose flour
1 (14-oz.) can chicken broth
½ cup water

4 med. potatoes, peeled and diced
(approx 4 cups)
1 cup milk
1 cup sliced green beans, partially
cooked
1 cup diced carrots
chopped fresh parsley

In a heavy skillet, brown sausage over medium heat. Remove sausage and set aside. Drain all but 1 tablespoon drippings. Sauté celery, onion, thyme and salt until onion is tender. Stir in flour. Cook 1 minute. Gradually add broth and water, stirring until mixture boils. Add potatoes. Cover and simmer for 25 minutes. Add milk, beans and sausage. Heat through. Garnish with parsley. Season with pepper or spices to your liking (garlic powder).

SOUTHWEST CHILI

Linda Heck

1 l-lb. chicken breast
1 med. onion
1½ tsp. garlic powder
1 T. vegetable oil
2 cans great northern beans (15 oz. can)
1 can chicken broth (14 oz.)
2 cans chopped green chilies (4 oz.)

1 tsp. salt
1 tsp. ground cumin
1 tsp. dried oregano
½ tsp. pepper
½ tsp. cayenne pepper
1 cup sour cream
½ cup whipping cream

In a large saucepan, sauté chicken, onion and garlic powder in oil until chicken is no longer pink. Add beans, broth, chilies and all of the seasonings. Bring to a boil. Reduce heat, simmer, uncovered for 30 minutes. Remove from heat, stir in sour cream and whipping cream. Serve immediately.

SPICY BLACK BEAN SOUP

Melissa Lesniewski

cooking spray (Pam)
1 med. onion, finely chopped
4 med. garlic cloves, minced
3 (15-oz.) cans black beans, undrained
½ tsp. red pepper flakes, or to taste

1 tsp. ground cumin
1 (14½ - oz.) can fat-free chicken broth or vegetable broth
1 (10-oz.) can tomatoes with green chilies
1 (11-oz.) can yellow corn, drained

Coat bottom of large stockpot with cooking spray. Add onion and garlic and cook, stirring frequently, until onions are soft but not brown, about 5 minutes. Place once can of beans in blender; add sautéed onion mixture, red pepper flakes and cumin. Cover and blend on high until smooth, about 30 seconds. Pour mixture back into stockpot. Place second can of beans and broth in blender and purée until smooth; add to stockpot. Stir third can of beans (do not purée first), tomatoes and green chilies, and corn into stockpot. Bring to a boil, lower heat to medium and simmer for 20-25 minutes. Yields about 1½ cups of soup per serving.

74987-06

SPICY SAUSAGE, BARLEY AND MUSHROOM STEW

Jennie Geisler
From the Erie Times–News

2 tsp. olive oil
2 cups onion, thinly sliced
8 oz. spicy turkey Italian sausage
1 cup celery, chopped
1 cup carrot, sliced
2 cloves garlic, minced
1 bay leaf
5 cups shiitake mushroom caps, thinly sliced
1½ cups portobello mushrooms, chopped

½ cup pearl barley, uncooked
6 cups fat-free, less sodium chicken broth
2 T. brandy
1 tsp. salt
¼ tsp. black pepper, freshly ground
⅓ cup fresh parsley, coarsely chopped

Heat oil in a large Dutch oven over medium heat. Add onion and cook 5 minutes, or until soft. Remove casings from sausage. Add sausage to pan, cook 8 minutes or until sausage is browned, stirring to crumble. Add celery, carrot, garlic and bay leaf. Cook 10 minutes or until onions are golden brown, stirring frequently. Stir in the mushrooms, cook 10 minutes or so until mushrooms release moisture. Stir in barley, chicken broth, brandy, salt and pepper. Bring to a boil, cover, and reduce heat. Simmer 1 hour or until barley is tender. Discard bay leaf. Sprinkle with parsley. Serve immediately. Preparation 15 minutes, cooking time 95 minutes. Makes 6 (1-cup) servings

Recipe Note: This is a favorite hearty cold-weather recipe of mine. It has so much flavor, you'll never notice how good it is for you. Per serving: 215 calories, 7.2 grams fat, 13.3 grams protein, 23.4 grams carbohydrates, 4.7 grams fiber, 27 milligrams cholesterol, 527 milligrams sodium

SPINACH SALAD

Rosemarie Pitetti

9 slices bacon, cut up
3 T. lemon juice
2 T. brown sugar
2 T. Dijon mustard

1 (10-oz.) pkg. fresh spinach, torn
1 (8-oz.) pkg. fresh mushrooms, sliced

Fry bacon until crisp. Drain. Reserve ¼ cup of bacon drippings. Add lemon juice, brown sugar, and mustard to the ¼ cup of bacon drippings. Cook over low heat stirring constantly for 1 minute. Toss spinach and mushrooms with this mixture. Sprinkle with bacon.

SPINACH-SALSA SOUP

Heather Cass

Erie
Times-News

4 cup chicken broth	I can kidney beans
I cup salsa	tortilla chips
1½ cup fresh baby spinach	shredded cheddar cheese

Bring chicken broth and salsa to a boil in a large saucepan. Add spinach and simmer until tender. Add kidney beans and heat through. Serve topped with crumbled tortilla chips and shredded cheddar cheese.

Recipe Note: I always use baked tortilla chips and fat-free or light cheese to cut calories and fat. Also, I love spinach so I always put in about twice the amount this recipe calls for.

STUFFED PEPPER SOUP

Sandy Reid

2½ lb. Meat loaf mix from Wegmans	I (26-28 oz.) can Red Pack diced, crushed unpeeled tomatoes
¾ cup chopped Vidalia onions	I (10¾ oz.) can Campbell's tomato soup
2 chopped green peppers	
2 cloves minced garlic	3 (14-oz.) cans Swanson's beef broth OR good bullion
2 tsp. salt	
2 tsp. fresh ground pepper	I pinch baking soda
2 cup instant rice, uncooked	grated Parmesan cheese

Brown ground meat in a stock pot; add onion, peppers, garlic, salt and pepper. Ground meat should be browned and onions and peppers slightly soft. Add instant rice, tomatoes and tomato soup. Mix well. Add beef broth and baking soda. Simmer for 45 minutes to I hour. Top with grated Parmesan cheese and serve with crusty bread.

Recipe Note: Instead of simmering for 45 minutes, I like to put all of the ingredients in a large crock pot on low for a few hours. This soup travels well and is great on a buffet. Leftovers can be frozen for use at a later date.

74987-06

SUMMER PASTA SALAD

Mary Ann Yonko

1-lb. box small shell pasta
½ lb. provolone (cut into small pieces)
¼ lb. hard salami (cut into small pieces)
½ lb. pepperoni (cut into small pieces)
½ lb. ham (cut into small pieces)
3 stalks celery, chopped

1 sm. red onion, chopped
1 cup black olives, sliced
½ cup green olives, sliced
½ green pepper, chopped
1 can chi chi (garbanzo) beans, drained
3 plum tomatoes (cut into small pieces)

Dressing

1½ tsp. salt
1 tsp. oregano
1 tsp. pepper

1 cup oil
¾ cup wine vinegar

Cook pasta to package directions. Mix together. Add plum tomatoes right before serving. Serves lots!

Recipe Note: Best if made day ahead or early day of.

SWEET AND SOUR SALAD

Phoebe Wood

1 lb. shells, cooked
1 cucumber, sliced
1 green pepper, chopped
1 onion, chopped
1 small jar pimentos, drained

1 can tomato soup
¾ cup sugar
¾ cup vinegar
¾ cup salad oil

Mix all liquid ingredients together with sugar. Reserve 1 cups of this mixture. Pour rest of liquid on all other ingredients. Pour remaining cup on just before serving. Best if let stand in refrigerator several hours before serving

TACO SALAD

Jennifer Wright

1 lb. beef
1 small onion
1 pkt. taco seasoning
1 large bottle Catalina salad dressing

1 bag Doritos
2 tomatoes
sliced black olives
2 cup shredded cheddar cheese
1 head lettuce

Cook beef and onion. Add taco seasoning according to package. Let cool. Shred lettuce, cut tomatoes and olives and mix into beef mixture. Crush Doritos. Add Doritos and dressing before serving for best results.

Recipe Note: I'm sure you could use low-fat everything and even use turkey burger!

TEX-MEX BEAN STEW

Heather Cass

Erie
Times-News

1 cup salsa
1 cup barbecue sauce
1 pkt. taco seasoning mix
1 (15-oz.) can corn

1 (15-oz.) can chickpeas, rinsed
1 (15-oz.) can black beans, rinsed
1½ lb. lean beef chunks

Mix all ingredients, except beans, in a slow cooker. Cover and cook on high for 4 to 5 hours or on low for 8 to 10 hours until beef is very tender. Stir in beans. Cover; let stand 5 minutes for beans to heat through.

Recipe Note: I usually make this stew without the meat and it's still delicious. To add some heat, opt for hot taco seasoning or throw in some red pepper flakes.

THREE BEAN SALAD

JoAnne Bruno

⅔ cup vinegar
⅓ cup salad oil
¾ cup sugar
1 tsp. salt
½ tsp. black pepper
1 can yellow wax beans, drained

1 can green beans, drained
1 can kidney beans, drained
1 can chick peas, drained, optional
½ cup thinly sliced onion
½ cup thinly sliced green peppers

Mix thoroughly vinegar, oil, sugar, salt and pepper. Pour over mixture of beans, onions and peppers in a large bowl. Mix gently. Cover and refrigerate overnight. Mix well before serving.

TOMATO BASIL BOWTIE SALAD

Sherry Rieder

2 cups chopped plum tomatoes
¼ cup fresh basil, cut into strips
  (or 1 tsp. dried) (fresh is much
  better)
1 T. canola oil
1 T. red wine vinegar

2 cloves garlic, minced
1 tsp. salt
6 oz. bowtie pasta, cooked al
  dente
fresh ground pepper, to taste

Combine everything but the pasta. Pour it over the pasta and mix. Add fresh black pepper to taste.

74987-06

TURKEY CHILI

Sherry Rieder

1 lb. smoked turkey breast, cubed
1 jar picante sauce
1 can pinto beans, rinsed and
   drained
1 can kidney beans, rinsed and
   drained

1 can black beans, rinsed and
   drained
2 (14-oz.) cans stewed tomatoes
2 T. chili powder
1 can corn, drained
2 tsp. lime juice

Combine all ingredients, except lime juice. Heat until bubbling. Add lime juice just before serving.

TURKEY SOUP

Mary Agnes Mosher

1 cup chopped turkey (or more!)
¼ cup finely chopped onion
¼ cup butter
2 cup diced, raw red potatoes
2 cup turkey or chicken broth
2 stalks celery, sliced

1 (13-oz.) can evaporated milk
2 T. chopped parsley
1 tsp. salt
¼ tsp. ginger
¼ tsp. paprika
⅛ tsp. pepper

Sauté onion in butter. Stir in remaining ingredients and cook over medium heat for 20-25 minutes or until potatoes are cooked.

Recipe Note: Great for leftover turkey at Thanksgiving!

VEGETABLE BURGER SOUP
(very easy)

Cindy Hickernell
From Barbara Hann

1 lb. ground beef or turkey, fried
   out and drained
1 (20-oz.) pkg. frozen mixed
   vegetables
1 (29-oz.) can crushed tomatoes

1 (15-oz.) can tomato sauce
4 cups water
1 envelope dry onion soup
2 tsp. sugar

Combine all ingredients and cook for at least one hour. Can be made in crockpot. Can also be made without meat.

Recipe Note: Fry up a quantity of ground meat ahead of time, drain and freeze portions for use in this or other recipes.

WHITE BEAN CHICKEN CHILI

Melissa Lesniewski

Erie
Times-News

1 med. onion
3 T. olive oil
(4-oz.) Old El Paso peeled,
 chopped green chilies
3 T. all-purpose flour
2 tsp. ground cumin

1 (32-oz.) can great northern
 beans or white beans
1 (14½ - oz.) can chicken broth
1½ cups chopped cooked chicken
 (or 2 large cans of cooked all-
 white meat chunks)

Finely chop onion. In large skillet, cook onion in oil for 4 minutes or until transparent. Add chilies, flour and cumin. Cook and stir for 2 minutes. Add beans and chicken broth. Bring to a boil. Reduce heat and simmer for 10 minutes or until thickened. Add chicken and cook until hot.

Recipe Note: Chili is not spicy at all since the canned green chilies are very mild. I add 1 tsp. chili powder to give it a little more kick or you can pass the Tabasco sauce and let everybody season it to their own taste.

Recipe Favorites

74987-06

VEGETABLES & SIDE DISHES

BAKED BEANS

Sara Simpson

1 (15-oz.) can pork and beans,
  undrained
1 (15-oz.) can barbeque beans,
  undrained
1 (15-oz.) can kidney or pinto
  beans, undrained
1 (15-oz.) can butter beans, drained
1 (15-oz.) can white or navy beans,
  drained

1 lb. bacon, cut into 1-inch pieces
3/4 cup brown sugar, packed
1/2 cup white vinegar
1/4 cup dried instant minced onion
1 tsp. dry mustard
1 tsp. garlic salt

Combine all ingredients in 3½ quart casserole. Bake uncovered at
350 degrees for 2½ - 3 hours. Serves 10-20.

BAKED EGGPLANT

Judy Lohse

1/3 - 1/2 cup mayonnaise or salad
  dressing
1 med. eggplant, sliced into 1/4"
  slices lengthwise

1/3 cup saltine crackers, crushed
  (or Japanese panko bread
  crumbs)
1/3 cup grated Parmesan cheese

Spread mayonnaise on both sides of sliced eggplant. Dip into crumb-
cheese mixture. Bake on oiled pan and spray with Pam on top. Bake
in preheated 400 degree oven until golden and crispy, approximately
15-20 minutes. Serve with more Parmesan if desired.

Recipe Note: Fast and Easy! Serves 4. Love this recipe especially with
panko crumbs.

BAKED LIMA BEANS

Phoebe Wood

2 pkgs. lima beans
2½ cup granulated sugar
2 tsp. salt

1 tsp. dry mustard
1/2 cup ketchup
bacon

Cook the lima beans and drain. Add all other ingredients and cook
slowly. Place in casserole dish and put bacon on top. Flip bacon
while baking.

BAKED PINEAPPLE

Terri Michalski

1 can crushed pineapple
¾ cup sugar
2 T. cornstarch, mixed with ¼ c. water

2 eggs, beaten
1 tsp. vanilla
butter
cinnamon

Mix all ingredients in 1-quart casserole dish. Sprinkle top with pieces of butter and cinnamon. Bake at 350 degrees for 1 hour.

BAKED PINEAPPLE

Mandy Barney

2 eggs (beaten)
3 rounded T. minute tapioca

¾ cup sugar
1 (16-oz.) can crushed pineapple

Mix all ingredients together. Top with cinnamon. Bake 350 degrees for ½ hour.

BAKED PINEAPPLE CASSEROLE

Nancy Group

1 cup sugar
½ cup margarine
4 eggs at room temperature

1 can crushed pineapple with liquid
3 slices bread, cubed

Melt margarine. Beat eggs. Mix all ingredients together in a greased casserole. Bake for 1 hour at 350 degrees. Great to serve with ham.

BUTTERNUT SQUASH BAKE

Betty Smulik

⅓ cup butter or margarine, softened
1 can evaporated milk
2 cups mashed cooked butternut squash
¾ cup sugar

2 eggs
1 tsp. vanilla
½ cup rice cereal
¼ cup chopped pecans
¼ cup packed brown sugar
2 T. butter or margarine, melted

In a mixing bowl cream butter and sugar. Beat in eggs, milk and vanilla. Stir in squash. Pour into a greased 11x7 baking pan. Bake uncovered at 350 degrees for 45 minutes or until almost set. Sprinkle topping mix over squash. Return to oven 5-10 minutes or until bubbly. Topping mix consists of the last 4 ingredients on the list.

74987-06

CHEESE CHILE CORN CASSEROLE

Dannielle Zygai Hunt
Jackie Hunt

2 (10-oz.) cans whole kernel corn
1 (10-oz.) can creamed style corn
1 (8-oz.) can diced green chilies
1 (8-oz.) pkg. cream cheese

Add all ingredients to large microwave safe bowl, or sauce pan. Heat until cream cheese melts and casserole is hot, stirring intermittently.

Recipe Note: Using low-fat cream cheese makes little difference in the flavor of this dish, so feel free to save some calories, without compromising the taste!

CHEESY POTATO PUFF

Jane (Rohleder) Voltz

12 medium potatoes, peeled and
  cubed
2 cups cheddar, Colby or Swiss
  cheese, divided
1¼ cups milk
⅓ cup butter or margarine,
  softened
1-2 tsp. salt
2 large eggs, beaten

Place the potatoes in a saucepan; cover with water. Place lid on saucepan and bring to a boil. Cook until tender, about 15 to 20 minutes. Drain and mash. Add 1¾ cups cheese, milk, butter, and salt. Cook and stir over low heat until cheese and butter are melted. Fold in eggs; Spread into a greased 13 x 9 x 2 baking dish. Bake, uncovered at 350 degrees for 25 to 30 minutes. Sprinkle with the remaining cheese. Bake about 5 minutes longer or until golden brown. Yield: 12-14 servings.

CHEESY POTATOES

Peg Hess

2 cups Hellmann's mayonnaise
1 lb. Velveeta
2 lbs. frozen hash browns

Melt Hellmann's and cheese in microwave. Mix in potatoes. Bake uncovered at 350 degrees for 1 to 1½ hours.

CHINESE BROCCOLI

Sandy Reid

2 bunches broccoli   water for blanching

Cut flowerets from broccoli. Peel stems and slice diagonally. Put the broccoli in boiling water for three minutes. Remove from hot water and drench with cold water. Chill.

SAUCE

2 T. sesame seeds   2 T. vegetable oil
2 T. soy sauce   ½ tsp. salt
2 T. vinegar   1 T. sugar

Toast sesame seed in a small bare pan over low to medium heat until brown. Slowly add soy sauce, vinegar, oil, salt and sugar to toasted sesame seeds. Combine and chill. When ready to serve, pour dressing over chilled broccoli.

Recipe Note: This is a great side dish with the Oriental Cornish hens.

CHINESE COLESLAW

Betty Smulik

1 head cabbage   2 T. sesame seeds
5 sliced green onions   1 cup sugar
1 stick oleo   1 cup vegetable oil
¼ cup regular onions   ½ cup vinegar
2 pkgs. ramen noodles   2 T. soy sauce

Brown stick of oleo and regular onions. Fry oleo, noodles, sesame seeds and sliced green onions. When cooled add noodle mixture to cabbage with browned onions and oleo mixture and dressing about 15 minutes before serving. Mix last 4 ingredients together to make dressing.

COUSRICTEA

Terry Dollivar

1 cup cooked couscous   ½ cup cooked rice
½ cup raisins   2 cups brewed green tea

Combine all ingredients. Serve.

74987-06

CURRIED FRUIT

Peggy Paul

1 can peach halves
1 can pear halves
2 cans pineapple chunks
⅓ cup melted butter

⅔ cup brown sugar
2½ tsp. curry powder
3 T. cornstarch

Drain fruit. Place hollow side up in a shallow baking dish. Mix all other ingredients and spread over top. Back at 325 degrees for 1 hour. Serves 10.

Recipe Note: This is best when made in advance and reheated.

DRUNKEN BEANS

Patricia Guilford

6 slices bacon
1 large Bermuda onion
1 (32-oz.) can baked beans
2 T. brown sugar
1 tsp. Worcestershire sauce
1 tsp. dry mustard
1 T. regular mustard
1 lb. ground hamburger, cooked
  and drained

1 cup ketchup
1 tsp. molasses
3 tsp. white sugar
1 (8-oz.) can crushed pineapple
  with juice
3 T. rum
1 small can tomato paste

Mix all ingredients in a bean pot and put in a 350 degree oven uncovered for 1 hour. Serve.

FIRE & ICE WATERMELON SALSA

Jennie Geisler
From the Erie Times–News

3 cups chopped watermelon
½ orange bell pepper, chopped
½ yellow bell pepper, chopped
2 T. red wine vinegar

2 T. parsley or cilantro
1 T. chopped canned jalapeño
2 cloves garlic, pressed
salt to taste

Mix ingredients well in a large bowl and transfer to a serving dish.

GARY'S FRIED APPLES

Betty Smulik

4 T. butter or margarine
2 large sweet onions, sliced
5 apples

4 T. brown sugar
½ tsp. cinnamon

Melt butter in frying pan. Cook onions until translucent and slightly browned. Halve and quarter apples and clean out core. Slice each piece again and add to frying pan. Cover and cook until tender. Add brown sugar and cinnamon and stir. This goes with many meat dishes.

HATTIE'S CRANBERRY SAUCE
(a family favorite)

Cindy Hickernell
From Newark Star–Ledger

1 (12-oz.) pkg. cranberries, fresh or
  frozen
1 cup sugar
¾ cup water

½ cup cognac or brandy
2 T. sugar
¼ tsp. vanilla

In 3 quart microwavable casserole, combine cranberries, 1 cup sugar, water and ¼ cup cognac. Cover with lid or vented plastic wrap. Microwave on high 6 to 8 minutes (slightly more if berries are frozen), or until sugar dissolves and cranberries start to pop. Stir once during cooking. Uncover, stir in vanilla and remaining sugar and cognac. Let stand until cool. Store in refrigerator in a tightly covered container.

LOW-CAL FETTUCCINI

Barbara Valaitis

1 (12-oz.) pkg. fettuccini, cooked
½ cup margarine (melted)
1½ cups low-fat Parmesan cheese,
  grated

1 cup condensed skim milk
¼ tsp. parsley

Mix all ingredients together. Add crushed bacon, cooked shrimp, or leftover chicken, beef or turkey.

74987-06

MEDITERRANEAN STUFFED PORTOBELLO MUSHROOMS

Maggie Wilson

2 large portobello mushroom caps
2 T. pine nuts
1 med. tomato, cored and diced
1 clove garlic, finely minced
1 T. fresh oregano, finely diced

2 T. fresh basil leaves, finely diced
4-6 pitted Kalamata olives, chopped
1/4 cup fresh baby spinach, diced
1 T. extra virgin olive oil

Begin by removing stem from underside of mushrooms. Gently remove dark gills using a small spoon to create room for the filling. Set aside. Using a small pan set over medium heat, toast pine nuts until lightly golden brown and slightly fragrant (2-3 minutes). Keep the nuts moving in the pan using a wooden spoon or by moving the pan around over the flame. Do not allow nuts to get overly brown. Set aside to cool. In a small bowl, add the diced tomato, garlic, oregano and basil, Kalamata olives and baby spinach and olive oil. Stir gently to combine. Dice pine nuts carefully and add to mixture. Fill each mushroom cap with stuffing and place over a gas or charcoal grill set on medium high for 6-8 minutes until mushrooms are soft to the touch and are no longer overly firm. Mushrooms can also be baked in a 375-degree oven for 10-15 minutes.

Recipe Note: Options: Many variations are possible. Add in Parmesan and mozzarella cheeses or artichokes if desired. Bread crumbs can also be added for a firmer texture.

NUTTY BROCCOLI SLAW

Caroline Mulson

1 (3-oz.) pkg. chicken-flavored ramen noodles
1 (16-oz.) pkg. broccoli/cabbage slaw mixture
2 cups sliced green onions, about 2 bunches
1½ cups broccoli florets

1 (6-oz.) can ripe black olives, drained and halved
1 cup sunflower kernels, toasted
½ cup slivered almonds, toasted
½ cup sugar
½ cup cider vinegar
½ cup olive oil

Set aside the noodle seasoning packet; crush the noodles and place in a large bowl. Add the slaw mix, onions, broccoli, olives, sunflower kernels and almonds. In a jar with a tight fitting lid, combine the sugar, vinegar, oil and contents of the seasoning packet; shake well. Drizzle over salad and toss to coat. Serve immediately. Yield 16 servings

ORANSQUAH

Terry Dollivar

1 cup cooked yellow squash 1 cup hominy
1 cup jellied cranberries

Erie
Times-News

Combine all ingredients. Serve.

OVEN ROASTED POTATOES

Brenda Williams

4 large potatoes 1 tsp. dried herbs (oregano, basil
4 T. butter or margarine or Italian blend
salt and pepper to taste

Largely dice potatoes and place in baking dish then add butter or margarine and seasonings. Bake approximately 30 minutes at 400 degrees until potatoes are softened.

PINEAPPLE CASSEROLE

Mary Agnes Mosher

2 (20-oz.) cans pineapple chunks 8 oz. sharp cheddar cheese,
or tidbits, drained shredded
1 cup sugar 1 pkg. Ritz crackers, crushed
5 T. flour 1 stick butter or margarine

Spray baking pan with Pam. Blend flour and sugar. Making 2 layers, layer ingredients (except butter) in order given. Pour melted butter over top. Bake at 350 degrees for 30 minutes until bubbling hot.

Recipe Note: Great served with ham or turkey at holiday dinners!

POTATO CASSEROLE

Marnie Mead Oberle

8 large potatoes, cubed ¼ cup onion, grated
1 cup Hellmann's mayonnaise 2-4 dashes hot sauce
1 cup Velveeta, cubed 1 cup seasoned bread crumbs
12 slices bacon, crumbled ¼ cup melted butter

Boil potatoes until a fork comes out tender, about 15 minutes. Mix with mayo, cheese (I sometimes mix in some cheddar to the Velveeta), bacon, onion and hot sauce. Put in 9x13 baking dish. Top with bread crumbs and pour butter on top. Bake at 350 degrees for 60 minutes.

74987-06

SAUTÉED RED CABBAGE

Pat Rhone

2 T. extra virgin olive oil
1 small onion. sliced
½ head red cabbage, shredded
⅓ cup white or apple cider
  vinegar

2 T. sugar
1 tsp. mustard seed
salt
pepper

Heat skillet over medium/high heat. Add oil and onion, sauté for 2 minutes. Add cabbage and turn in pan sautéing until it wilts, 3-5 minutes. Add vinegar to pan and turn cabbage in it. Sprinkle the sugar over the cabbage and turn again. Season with mustard seed, salt and pepper and reduce heat. Continue to cook 10 minutes or until ready to serve, stirring occasionally.

STUFFING BALLS

Phoebe Wood

6 cups bread crumbs
½ cup celery, chopped
½ cup onion, chopped
1½ sticks oleo
1 can cream of chicken soup

1 egg
½ cup water
1 tsp. salt
1 tsp. poultry seasoning

Simmer celery and onion in oleo until melted. Mix all ingredients together. Form into balls and bake uncovered on a cookie sheet. Bake at 350 degrees for 20 minutes. Makes 20 balls.

SUMMER BAKED BEANS

Dawn Blackburn

1 lb. diced bacon
1 lb. ground beef
2 large chopped onions
4 (15-oz.) cans pork and beans
1 (16-oz.) bottle honey BBQ sauce
1 (15-oz.) can kidney beans,
  drained

1 (15-oz.) can black beans, drained
1 (15-oz.) can lima beans, drained
½ cup brown sugar
3 T. cider vinegar
1 tsp. salt
½ tsp. black pepper

Cook bacon until slightly crisp and drain. Brown ground beef and onions in 5 quart. Dutch oven. Drain. Add the bacon with the rest of the ingredients and bake for 1 hour at 350 degrees.

SWEET POTATO CASSEROLE

JoAnne Bruno

2 eggs
3¼ cups cooked sweet potatoes, mashed
¼ cup butter, melted
1 cup sugar
1 tsp. vanilla extract

¼ cup milk
1 cup light brown sugar
½ cup flour
⅓ cup butter or margarine, softened
1 cup chopped pecans

Preheat oven to 350 degrees. In a large bowl beat eggs slightly. Add the sweet potatoes, butter, sugar, vanilla and milk. Blend well. Pour into a lightly buttered 3 quart casserole dish. In a separate bowl combine the rest of the ingredients and sprinkle on top of casserole. Bake uncovered for 45-55 minutes.

SWISS VEGETABLE MEDLEY

Paula Bendure

2 (16-oz.) bags frozen broccoli, cauliflower and carrot blend, thawed and drained
1 (10¾-oz.) can condensed cream of mushroom soup

1 cup shredded Swiss cheese
⅓ cup sour cream
¼ tsp. ground black pepper
1 (6-oz.) can French-fried onions

Combine vegetables, soup, ½ cup Swiss cheese, sour cream, black pepper and ½ can onions in large bowl. Pour into 2 quart casserole dish. Bake covered at 350 degrees for 30 minutes or until bubbling. Top with remaining ½ cup cheese and onions, bake for uncovered for another 5 minutes or until onions are light golden brown. 8-10 servings

Recipe Note: This side dish has been made by my mother for years during Thanksgiving dinner. It goes great with any meat dish and can be doubled for a larger party.

74987-06

TOMATO AND BASIL PIE

Jennie Geisler
From the Erie Times–News

1 9-inch pie crust
1½ cups reduced-fat mozzarella
  cheese, shredded
4 medium tomatoes
1 cup loosely packed fresh basil
  leaves, plus more for garnish

4 cloves garlic
½ cup Hellmann's light
  mayonnaise
¼ cup grated reduced-fat
  Parmesan cheese
⅛ tsp. ground white pepper

Preheat oven to 375 degrees. Unroll the pie crust, and place in a 9-inch quiche or pie plate. Flute the edges or press with fork tines. Pre-bake according to the package directions. Remove from oven and sprinkle with 1 cup of the mozzarella cheese. Cool on a wire rack. Cut tomatoes into wedges, and drain on paper towels. Arrange the wedges on top of the melted cheese in the baked shell. Chop basil and mince garlic, sprinkling over the tomatoes. In a medium mixing bowl, combine the remaining mozzarella cheese, mayonnaise, Parmesan and pepper. Spoon cheese mixture over basil mixture, spreading to evenly cover the top. Bake 35 to 40 minutes, or until the top is golden and bubbly. Serve warm garnished with basil leaves.

Recipe Note: Of all the recipes I've had in the paper in the past five years, I think this might be my favorite. Per serving: 250 calories, 16 grams of fat, 1 gram fiber.

TOMATO PIE

Susie Scott

1 (8-oz.) can Pillsbury refrigerated
  crescent dinner rolls
2 to 4 tsp. olive oil
½ cup chopped fresh basil

1-3 tsp. minced garlic
8 oz. provolone cheese, sliced
¼ cup grated Parmesan cheese
2-3 large tomatoes, sliced

Heat oven to 375 degrees. Lightly spray 10-inch pie pan with nonstick cooking spray. Separate dough into 4 equal sections. Press evenly over bottom and up sides of pan; firmly press to seal perforations. Prick dough with fork and cook for 10-15 minutes. Meanwhile, in small saucepan, heat oil (may use more if desired), basil and garlic. Cook over low heat just until heated; cover to keep warm. Arrange half of the provolone slices over partially baked crust; top with half the tomatoes. Sprinkle with half the Parmesan; repeat layer. Sprinkle basil mixture over pie. Bake at 375 for 15-18 minutes until cheese is melted and crust is a deep golden brown. Let stand 5 minutes; cut into wedges and serve.

Recipe Note: This is a great summer dish, when tomatoes taste the best. Everyone loves this dish!

TUNA CHEESE BALL
(You'll love it even if you don't like tuna!)

Tami Carrara

1 (3-oz.) can water-packed tuna
(drained)
1 (8-oz.) pkg. cream cheese

1 (3-oz.) pkg. chopped walnuts
onion salt to taste

Mix tuna, cream cheese and onion salt (don't leave out the onion salt!). Roll into a ball. Pour nuts on a plate and roll the ball in the nuts until covered. Chill or eat at room temperature with crackers. Delicious!

Recipe Note: These ingredients are easy to have on hand at all times for a spur of the moment snack. It tastes just as good at room temperature as it does chilled. Guests just rave about it!

VEGETABLE CURRY

Dawn Blackburn

½ head cauliflower, cut into
florets
1 med. eggplant, peeled and cubed
2 med. potatoes, cubed
3 T. vegetable oil
1 tsp. mustard seed

½ tsp. Old Bay seasoning
1 tsp. curry powder
1 tsp. salt
¼ cup water
1 tomato, chopped
1 T. lemon juice

Cook the cauliflower until it is crisp tender, drain well. Boil potatoes until soft, drain. Heat oil in a large heavy pan with a lid. Add mustard seed and brown, covered, but be careful not to burn. Stir in the Old Bay, curry powder and salt. Add the cauliflower and stir well to coat. Add the eggplant and the water. Cook a few minutes and then add the potatoes. Continue to cook over medium high heat until flavors are well blended, adding more water a tablespoon at a time if needed. Add the tomatoes and lemon juice and serve immediately. Cooking time depends on how crispy you like your vegetables.

ZUCCHINI APPETIZER/CASSEROLE
Eileen Kloecker Perino

3 cups shredded zucchini
1 cup Bisquick
½ cup aged Romano cheese
½ cup chopped onion
2 T. parsley
½ tsp. salt

½ tsp. seasoned salt
½ tsp. oregano
1 dash pepper
½ tsp. garlic powder
½ cup vegetable oil
4 lg. eggs, beaten

Mix all ingredients in bowl. Pour into 9x13 (or 8x11 for thicker pieces) Bake at 350 degrees for 30 minutes.

Recipe Note: Very quick and easy. Crowd pleaser. Can be a simple meal or side dish or appetizer. It's addictive!

74987-06

ZUCCHINI PIE

Debra Hull

5 cups peeled and thinly sliced
  zucchini
¾ cup sugar
¼ cup lemon juice
¾ tsp. cinnamon
½ cup water

1 pie shell
1 cup flour
¾ cup brown sugar
½ tsp. salt
1 tsp. baking powder
6 T. soft butter

Combine zucchini, sugar, lemon juice, cinnamon, and water. Bring to a boil and cook about 15 minutes until zucchini looks clear. Bake pie shell for 8-10 minutes. Remove from oven. Put zucchini mixture into shell. Spoon liquid into zucchini until shell is covered. Discard unused. Mix the rest of the ingredients until crumbly. Spread on top of zucchini. Bake at 350 degrees for 45 minutes. Cool. Can be served with whipped topping.

Recipe Favorites

Erie
Times-News

MAIN DISHES

ARROZ CON POLLO
(Cuban-Style Rice with Chicken)

Maureen Bemko

8 chicken thighs
1 tsp. red pepper flakes
1 tsp. ground cumin
1 tsp. chili powder
1 tsp. salt
½ tsp. freshly ground pepper
3 T. olive oil (divided use)
1 med. onion, chopped
3 cloves garlic, chopped
1 cup low-salt, low-fat chicken broth
½ cup roasted red bell pepper, chopped
1 (15-oz.) can plum tomatoes, chopped
¾ cup canned black beans, rinsed
1 (15-oz.) can baby corn, drained
¼ tsp. salt
½ cup long-grain rice, preferably basmati
2 T. fresh cilantro, chopped
¼ cup low-fat sour cream
1 ripe avocado, peeled and quartered

Skin chicken thighs. Combine next 5 ingredients and rub onto chicken; cover and refrigerate for at least 1 hour or overnight. In heavy Dutch oven, heat 2 tablespoons olive oil and sauté chicken on all sides about 5 minutes. Remove chicken and set aside. Add remaining tablespoon of oil to Dutch oven and sauté onion and garlic for 3 minutes or till translucent. Stir in chicken broth, roasted red bell pepper, tomatoes with juice, black beans, baby corn, and salt. Bring to simmer; return chicken to Dutch oven. Cover and reduce heat to low; cook 20 minutes. Add rice; turn chicken pieces over and cook another 15 minutes. Stir up rice from bottom, add cilantro, and cook 5 more minutes. Transfer rice mixture and chicken to platter or individual plates; garnish with avocado quarter, placing a tablespoon of sour cream into the curve of each avocado quarter. Serves 4.

Recipe Note: This delicious dish is a modified version of Virtual Kitchen's arroz con pollo. Pair it with a green salad, and dinner is done. For those who prefer milder flavors, the cook may omit the red pepper flakes from the spice rub.

ASPARAGUS STIR FRY

Heather Cass

1 lb. fresh asparagus
1 tsp. cornstarch
1 T. water
1 T. soy sauce
1 T. vegetable oil

4 green onions, sliced
2 cups mushrooms, sliced
2 tomatoes, cut into chunks
2 cups rice, cooked

Snap off base and slice asparagus into 2-inch lengths. In small bowl, blend water and cornstarch. Stir in soy sauce and set aside. Stir-fry asparagus and green onions in oil for about 4 minutes. Add mushrooms and cook another minute. Stir and push vegetables to the sides; add cornstarch sauce. Simmer for a minute, then stir in tomatoes and vegetables; heat through. Serve with cooked rice.

Recipe Note: Sprinkle toasted sesame seeds on top for a little something extra.

BARBECUE HAM SANDWICH

Mary Ann Yonko

1½ lbs. shaved ham
⅓ cup chopped onion
3 T. margarine
1 cup ketchup
¼ cup cider vinegar

2 T. brown sugar
½ cup water
2 tsp. mustard
2 T. Worcestershire sauce

Simmer for 10 minutes and serve on buns.

BARBECUE PORK CHOPS

Jean Hughes

4-6 center cut pork chops
½ cup chopped onions
½ cup brown sugar
½ cup ketchup

6 T. vinegar
2 T. Worcestershire sauce
salt & pepper to taste

Boil all ingredients for 1 minute; pour over chops (9x13 pan) and bake at 350 degrees (covered with foil) for about 1 hour or until fork tender.

Recipe Note: Thicker chops may require longer cooking time - use discretion.

BEEF PAPRIKA

Jade Conners
Cam Berquist – Mom

¼ cup Crisco
2 lb. beef tips - 1-inch cubes
½ cup c. sliced onion
½ tsp. minced garlic
¾ cup ketchup
2 T. Worcestershire sauce

1 T. brown sugar
2 tsp. salt
2 tsp. paprika
½ tsp. dry mustard
1½ cup water
dash cayenne pepper

Mix together in frying pan. Simmer 1 hour or until meat is tender.

THICKENER

2 tsp. flour   ¼ cup water

At end, mix flour and water and add to pan. This will thicken the sauce. Serve over egg noodles.

BEER CAN CHICKEN

Jennie Geisler
From the Erie Times–News

**Erie
Times-News**

¼ cup coarse salt
¼ cup dark brown sugar, packed
¼ cup sweet paprika
2 T. freshly ground black pepper
1 (12-oz.) can beer

1 3½- to 4-pound chicken
2 tsp. vegetable oil
2 cups wood chips, soaked in
 water or beer

Combine the first four ingredients and set aside. This is the rub you'll need to flavor the bird before cooking. Pop the tab off the beer can and pour half of it over the soaking wood chips. Using a church key-style can opener, make 2 additional holes in its top. Set the can of beer aside. Remove and discard the packet of giblets and the fat from just inside the body and neck cavities. Rinse the chicken, inside and out, under cold water and drain and blot dry with paper towels. Sprinkle 1 teaspoon of the rub inside the body cavity and ½ teaspoon inside the neck cavity of the chicken. Drizzle the oil over the outside of the bird and rub or brush it all over the skin. Spread 1 tablespoon of rub all over the skin. Spoon 1½ teaspoons of rub into the beer through the hole in the top of the can. The beer will foam up. Hold the bird with the opening of the body cavity at the bottom, and lower it onto the beer can, so the can fits into the cavity. Preheat the grill to medium and place soaked wood chips into smoker box and onto coals for gas grills or put the wood chips directly on the coals for charcoal grills. Stand the chicken up in the middle of the grate and cover, cooking 1 to 1½ hours, or until meat registers 180 degrees on a meat thermometer. The skin will turn very dark and crisp. If using a charcoal grill, you'll need to add 12 fresh coals per side after 1 hour. If the chicken starts to brown too much, tent the bird with aluminum foil. Using tongs, hold the bird by the can and carefully transfer it in an upright position onto a platter. Let the chicken rest for 5 minutes, then carefully lift it off its support. Take care not to spill the hot beer or otherwise burn yourself. Carve and serve. Store the remaining rub in an airtight container for up to 6 months.

Recipe Note: Making this recipe was some of the most fun I've had writing my column. It's from "Beer-Can Chicken and 74 other Offbeat Recipes for the Grill," by Steven Raichlen.

74987-06

CHICKEN & PORK ALMONDINE

Judy Fritz

1 pkg. Uncle Ben's wild rice
1 lb. bulk pork sausage
1 med. onion, chopped
1 clove garlic, finely chopped
1 stalk celery, finely chopped
1 cup slivered almonds

1 (10¾-oz.) can cream of
 mushroom soup
¾ cup milk
3 whole chicken breasts, cooked
 and diced

Prepare rice according to package directions. Brown sausage, onions, garlic and celery. Drain off grease. Mix all ingredients together, adding ¾ cup milk and reserving ½ cup of almonds for top of casserole. Transfer mixture to a casserole dish and top with remaining almonds and a sprinkle of parsley. Bake at 350 degrees for 30 minutes or until bubbly. Serves 6.

Recipe Note: Elegant but simple!

CHICKEN AND BISCUITS

Evelyn and Dave Rieder

2 T. olive oil
1 pat butter
7 chicken breasts, with skin
1 (14-oz.) can chicken broth

1½ to 2 tsp. chicken base
2 cup hot water
2 T. cornstarch

In a large hot skillet, add olive oil and butter. Add chicken pieces and cook on medium heat until golden brown. Add broth and water. Cover and cook over medium-low for 30 minutes. Remove chicken from pan. Remove skin. Cut up chicken into small pieces. Add cornstarch to small amount of cold water, then add mixture to gravy still in pan. Add chicken base to gravy. Add chicken pieces to gravy. Cover and cook over low heat, 10 to 15 minutes. Add cornstarch to thicken, if needed. Add salt and pepper, to taste.

BISCUITS

2 cups flour
3 tsp. baking power
1 tsp. salt

¼ cup Crisco
1 cup milk

Combine flour, baking powder and salt in large bowl. Add Crisco by cutting it into dry ingredients with whisk. Don't overwork. Add milk. Mix slowly around edges, then whip vigorously. Spoon onto greased baking sheet. Bake 12 minutes at 450 degrees.

CHICKEN CASSEROLE/SANDWICH FILLING
Mandy Barney

2 cups chicken, cooked and diced   1 can cream of chicken soup
2 cups potato chips, crushed

Erie
Times-News

Put all ingredients in baking dish and bake at 350 degrees, 20-30 minutes or put ingredients in skillet on top of stove, heat and eat. Eat as main dish or put on sandwich rolls.

CHICKEN CORDON BLEU CASSEROLE
Judy Fritz

1 lb. cooked baby red potatoes,   8 oz. cooked ham, cut into ½-inch
  cut into 1-inch chunks   chunks
1 lb. cooked boneless chicken   2 cups shredded Swiss cheese
  breast, cut into 1-inch chunks   1 T. chopped parsley
2 cups cooked broccoli florets   1 finely chopped garlic clove
1 (10¾-oz.) can cream of chicken
  soup

Preheat oven to 350 degrees. Put all ingredients in a bowl and toss to mix well. Transfer into a 9x13 glass or ceramic baking dish. Bake casserole, uncovered, for 30 minutes or until bubbly. Makes 6 main-dish servings.

Recipe Note: Each serving is about 375 calories. This casserole really does taste like the 'real thing.'

CHICKEN ENCHILADAS
Marty Merritt

2 chicken breasts (boiled &   1 can green chilies (chopped)
  shredded or diced)   1 (4-oz.) pkg. cream cheese
2 T. butter or margarine   8 8" flour tortillas
1 med. onion (chopped)

Cook onion in butter until limp, but not brown. Add green chiles. Sauté. Add cooked chicken & cream cheese. Heat until cheese is melted. Heat tortillas in microwave for about 20 seconds (these need to be warm, but not hard). Spoon filling down center of each tortilla. Roll up & set seam-side down in greased 9x13 pan.

SAUCE

1 can cream of chicken soup   3 T. picante sauce or salsa
½ cup sour cream   grated cheddar cheese

Mix soup, sour cream & picante or salsa together. Pour over enchiladas. Sprinkle grated cheese over top. Cover with foil. Bake at 375 degrees for 20 minutes. Uncover and bake an additional 10-15 minutes. Serve with rice or salad (or both!). Serves 8.

74987-06

CHICKEN ENCHILADAS

Mary Ann Yonko

½ cup chopped onion
4 T. margarine
¼ cup flour
2 cups chicken broth
1 tsp. chicken bouillon powder
1 (8-oz.) carton sour cream

3 cups shredded cooked chicken
2 cups shredded cheddar cheese
1 (4-oz.) can drained, chopped
   green chili peppers
1 tsp. chili powder
12 tortillas

In saucepan sauté onion in margarine until tender. Add flour, chicken broth, and bouillon. Cook and stir until thickened. Remove from heat, stir in sour cream. In large bowl combine 1 cup of the cooked sauce, chicken, 1 cup cheese, chili peppers and powder. Mix well. Fill each tortilla with equal portions of chicken mixture. Roll up and arrange in greased 9x13 pan. Spoon remaining sauce over all and sprinkle with cheese. Bake at 350 degrees for 25 minutes.

CHICKEN TENDERS CASSEROLE

Donna Strong

8 boneless chicken breasts, cubed
2 eggs
milk
Italian bread crumbs
oil

2 T. butter
¾ lb. Muenster cheese, sliced
mushrooms, halved
2 cups chicken bouillon

Marinate chicken cubes in beaten eggs and milk to cover, for 2 hours in the refrigerator. Bread the cubes in bread crumbs and garlic salt if you wish. Brown in fry pain in oil. Melt butter in 9x13 baking dish. Layer chicken and put fresh mushrooms on, then Muenster cheese. Mix 1 cup hot water and bouillon cubes. Pour over chicken and bake uncovered 45 minutes at 350 degrees. Can be made ahead and refrigerated, but don't pour chicken broth on till ready to bake.

CHICKEN WALDORF SALAD

Sherry R. Letzelter

1 cup mayonnaise
2 T. milk
2 T. lemon juice
1 T. sugar
½ tsp. salt
1½ cups cooked macaroni

1 (11-oz.) can mandarin oranges,
   well drained
1 cup chopped celery
2 cups cooked, cubed chicken
1 red apple, diced

In a large bowl, stir together the first 5 ingredients. Add remaining items & toss to coat well. Cover and chill.

Recipe Note: Make ahead of time, ready to pull out of the refrigerator and eat whenever. My family requests this dish often, especially in the summer.

CHICKEN WITH ROSEMARY

Rich Forsgren

Erie
Times-News

¼ cup kosher salt
1½ T. light brown sugar
2 tsp. fresh rosemary, minced
½ T. ground pepper

3 cloves garlic, minced
1 tsp. vegetable oil
8 9-oz. chicken breasts, with bone
and skin

Combine all ingredients but chicken. Rub into chicken and refrigerate 20 to 40 minutes. Rinse. Grill on skin side 9 minutes, other side 7 minutes.

CHOW MEIN CHICKEN

Marge Curtis

PART 1

1 med. onion, chopped
2 stalks celery, chopped

¼ c. oleo or butter

Cook onion and celery in oleo or butter in a skillet over medium heat for 5 minutes or until soft.

PART 2

1 can cream of mushroom soup
⅓ cup chicken broth
1 can bean sprouts, drained

2 cup cooked chicken, shredded
½ tsp. soy sauce

Add ingredients to Part 1. Cook for 10 minutes, stirring often. Pour into casserole (greased).

TOPPING

1 cup chow mein noodles

⅓ cup cashews (optional)

Sprinkle ingredients onto casserole. Bake in preheated 350 degree oven for 30 minutes.

Recipe Note: To make it easier yet, I serve casserole with chicken Rice-A-Roni from a box. Everyone loves it and it's simple!

74987-06

COMPANY CHICKEN AND STUFFING CASSEROLE
Judy Lohse

4 whole chicken breasts, split,
  skinned and deboned
8 slices Swiss cheese
1 (10¾ oz.) can cream of
  mushroom soup (undiluted)
¼ cup white wine, such as
  Riesling

1½ cups herb-seasoned stuffing
  mix or 3 oz. chicken-flavored
  stuffing mix
¼ cup melted butter or
  margarine

Place chicken in a greased 9x13 dish. Top each breast with cheese. Combine soup and wine and spoon over the chicken. Drizzle butter over stuffing mix and place this mixture over all. Press stuffing mix down a little in the sauce. Bake 45 minutes, uncovered. If you need to use foil loosely, add another 15 minutes.

Recipe Note: A dependable, tasty favorite! I like to use sliced mushrooms on each breast and white Zinfandel occasionally. Make sure to mix the stuffing mix up a little, as the herbs tend to settle on the bottom of the box.

CURRIED BROCCOLI CHICKEN CASSEROLE
Maggie Wilson

4 cooked chicken breasts, meat
  shredded or diced
2 heads fresh broccoli
1 can cream of chicken soup
1½ cups mayonnaise

1 T. curry powder
1 clove garlic, minced
2 T. lemon juice
1½ cups cheddar cheese, shredded
cooking spray

Preheat oven to 350 degrees. Cut head of broccoli into bite-sized pieces. Peel tough skin off of stalk and dice into bite-sized pieces. Place broccoli and chicken into 9x13 casserole dish. In a medium saucepan, combine cream of chicken soup, mayonnaise, curry powder, garlic and lemon juice. Bring to a boil over low heat, stirring constantly. Pour soup mixture over chicken/broccoli mixture and top with shredded cheese. Bake at 350 degrees for 30 minutes until broccoli is cooked and cheese is melted and bubbly.

Recipe Note: A great comfort food dish that is even better as leftovers. Add cooked rice or other vegetables as variations.

EASY BEEF STROGANOFF

Nancy Phillips

Erie
Times-News

1 pkg. stroganoff noodles
2 T. butter or oleo
2 lb. sirloin steak, cut into small strips
1 (4-oz.) can mushrooms (reserve liquid)

3 T. flour
1 env. onion soup mix
2¼ cups water
½ cup sour cream

Cook noodles and drain. Melt margarine in large skillet and brown meat; add mushrooms. Remove from skillet. To pan drippings, stir flour and onion soup mix; gradually add water and reserved mushroom liquid. Return meat and mushrooms to skillet; simmer 10 minutes. Blend in sour cream and heat through - do not bring to boil. Serve over noodles.

EASY ZUCCHINI SKILLET

Rose Moorhead

1 lb. ground beef
3 med. zucchini, thin sliced
1 onion, diced
1 green pepper, diced
(8-oz.) mushrooms, sliced

1 tsp. black pepper
½ tsp. sweet basil
½ tsp. garlic powder
(16-oz.) tomato sauce (any variety)
(8-oz.) shredded cheddar cheese

Brown ground beef in large skillet. Drain and return into skillet with remaining ingredients, except cheese. Simmer 40 minutes. Stir occasionally. Sprinkle with cheddar cheese before serving.

ELEGANT CHICKEN

Peggy Paul

4 boneless, skinless chicken breasts, cut into bite size pieces
4 eggs, beaten
1 cup chicken broth
¼ cup wine and pan drippings

½ lb. fresh mushrooms
¾ cup grated Muenster cheese
Italian bread crumbs
butter

Soak chicken in eggs for 1 hour. Roll in Italian bread crumbs. Sauté in butter until brown. Layer chicken in casserole with remaining ingredients. Bake in a 350 degree oven for 30-45 minutes.

74987-06

ESCALOPES ALA CREME

Patricia Guilford

4 skinless, boneless chicken
  breasts
½ pt. sour cream

½ lb. green beans
½ lb. mushrooms

Cut chicken breasts into bite size pieces and cook in butter for about 10 minutes. Add rest of ingredients to pan, salt and pepper to taste and continue to cook for 20-30 minutes. Serves 4

FABULOUS FLANK STEAKS

Susie Scott

2 1-lb. flank steaks
¾ cup cooking oil
¾ cup soy sauce
½ cup red wine vinegar
⅓ cup fresh lemon juice

¼ to ½ cup snipped parsley
¼ cup Worcestershire sauce
3 cloves garlic, minced
1 tsp. salt
1 tsp. pepper

In a 13x9 pan, arrange flank steaks. Stir together the rest of the ingredients and pour over flank steaks. Cover and refrigerate overnight, turning steaks occasionally. Drain steaks and discard marinade. Cook over medium coals for 10 - 15 minutes for rare, 15 - 18 minutes for medium rare, or 18-20 minutes for medium. Slice across grain.

FIESTA MACARONI
(Quick and Easy)

Elizabeth Korb

1 box cooked elbow macaroni
1 1-lb. cooked hamburger
1 (12-oz.) can chili beans
1 (16-oz.) jar medium flavor salsa

1 (12-oz.) can corn (drained)
1 (9-oz.) box Velveeta cheese
1 med. sour cream

Cut cheese in small cubes, mix all ingredients in a 9x13 pan and bake for 30 minutes at 325 degrees. Stir until everything is cheesy. Top each serving with sour cream.

FILET OF HADDOCK

Peach McVey

2 lbs. fish

1 can cream of shrimp soup

Pour soup over fish and bake for 20 minutes at 350 degrees.

1½ cups Ritz crackers, crushed
½ tsp. onion, grated
½ tsp. Worcestershire sauce

¼ tsp. garlic salt
2-3 T. butter, melted

Put crumbs on top of fish after baking for 20 minutes. Bake an additional 30 minutes. Serves 4-6.

FRIED CABBAGE AND PIEROGIS

Betty Smulik

Erie
Times-News

5 T. olive oil
1 large sweet onion
½ head cabbage, chopped

1 13 ounce can mushrooms
4 T. butter
pierogis

Prepare pierogis first by placing in boiling water until they begin to float. Then set aside. Fry onions in olive oil until translucent and slightly brown. Add mushrooms. Add chopped cabbage and begin browning and stirring. A cover is needed at this point. It will help reduce the cabbage to about half. Layer pierogis on top of the cabbage mixture. Add butter to taste. Stir gently. Serves 3-4

GLAZED KIELBASA

Sandra Yonko

3 lbs. fully cooked kielbasa or
  smoked sausage

¾ cup packed brown sugar
1½ cups ginger ale

Prep time = 5 minutes. Cook time = 4 hours. I remove the casing from the kielbasa/sausage. Cut kielbasa/sausage into 1-inch chunks. Place sausage in 3-quart slow cooker, sprinkle with brown sugar and then pour ginger ale over top. Cover and cook on sow setting for about 4 hours.

Recipe Note: To trim fat, you could use fat-free or turkey sausage. Enjoy!

GOULASH

Mary Taylor

1 lb. macaroni, cooked
1 pkg. Sloppy Joe mix
1 large can stewed tomatoes
1 can tomato soup
1 (8-oz.) water
1 cup diced onions

1 cup diced peppers
1 small can mushrooms
1 T. sugar
¼ cup BBQ sauce
1 lb. ground beef

Brown ground beef, mushrooms, peppers and onions together. Combine with all other ingredients except macaroni. Bring to a boil then reduce to simmer for 15 minutes. Add macaroni and stir.

74987-06

GOURMET CHICKEN

Dee Madura

4 boneless chicken breasts, split
2 T. chopped onion
⅛ tsp. salt
⅛ tsp. Accent
¼ lb. butter

⅓ cup milk
2 eggs
1½ cups bread crumbs
vegetable oil

Pound chicken until 4-inches long and 6-inches wide. Sprinkle with onion, accent, and salt. Place ⅛ stick of butter in breast and roll folding edges in. Beat eggs and combine with milk. Dip chicken in egg and milk mixture and roll in bread crumbs. Deep fry in oil until golden brown and crisp OR bake for 1 hour in the oven. Garnish with parsley. Serve.

GOURMET MUSHROOM FETTUCCINI

Kathleen Findlay

1 (4-oz.) pkg. fresh gourmet blend mushrooms: sliced crimini, shitake and oyster
1 pkg. fettuccini Florentine (spinach)

4 T. extra virgin olive oil
3 to 4 cloves garlic, minced
½ c. pine nuts
1 (3-oz.) pkg. sun-dried tomatoes, softened and minced

Cook fettuccini according to the instructions on the package. In a medium saucepan, heat the oil, and then sauté remaining ingredients for approx. 5 minutes. Remove from heat. Toss with the hot cooked fettuccini. Yield 6 servings.

Recipe Note: This quick, easy and healthful, palate-pleasing dish is a must for the mushroom lover!!

GREEK CHICKEN WITH ANGEL HAIR PASTA

Olivia Balczon

½ lb. cooked angel hair pasta
cooking spray (Pam)
4 boneless, skinless chicken breasts
2 cups red onion, chopped
1 cup yellow pepper, chopped

6 T. lemon juice
1 tsp. basil, dried
2 (14-oz.) cans diced tomato with basil, garlic and oregano
¾ cup crumbled feta cheese

Spray large skillet with cooking spray. Heat skillet and sauté chicken for 3 minutes each side. Add rest of ingredients except pasta and toss together and bring to a boil. Reduce heat, cover and simmer for 30 minutes or until done. Serve chicken breast with pasta and put ½ cup or a little more tomato mixture on top. Sprinkle with feta cheese. Serves 4.

GRILLED CHICKEN PASTA

Dana Kluz

Erie
Times-News

4 boneless, skinless chicken
  breasts
1 1-lb. box bowtie pasta, cooked
  and drained
1 bunch chopped scallions
1 med. can sliced black olives
1 carton cherry tomatoes, cut in
  half

1 bunch fresh basil, chopped
  coarsely
¾ cup olive oil
2 cups shredded Parmesan cheese
salt and pepper to taste

Prepare and marinade chicken at least 8 hours prior to cooking. Grill chicken and chop while hot. Cook pasta and drain. Toss pasta with fresh ingredients and olive oil. Add Parmesan cheese and toss. Top with warm chicken and serve. Can also be served chilled.

MARINADE

½ cup olive oil
⅓ cup Worcestershire sauce

⅓ cup soy sauce
2 to 3 cloves garlic, chopped

H.H. GRILLED PORK CHOPS

Mary Ann Yonko

4 pork chops
hickory Salt
2 T. Italian salad dressing
2 T. Worcestershire sauce
1 T. margarine
¼ cup honey

2 T. water
2 tsp. kitchen bouquet
1 T. hickory salt
1 dash pepper
1 dash garlic powder
1 dash onion salt

Sprinkle four large pork chops with meat tenderizer and hickory salt. Let sit in refrigerator for at least 30 minutes. Combine the rest of the ingredients on low heat until melted. Sear chops on both sides on hot grill. Baste often with sauce. Cook until juices run clear.

74987-06

HAM STUFFED MANICOTTI
Pat Rhone

8 manicotti shells
½ cup chopped onion
1 T. vegetable oil
3 cups fully cooked ham, ground
1 (4-oz.) can sliced mushrooms,
  drained
1 cup shredded Swiss cheese

3 T. grated Parmesan cheese
¼ cup chopped green pepper
3 T. butter or margarine
3 T. all-purpose flour
2 cups milk
paprika
freshly chopped parsley

Cook manicotti according to directions on package. Set aside. In large skillet, sauté onion in oil until tender. Remove from the heat. Add ham, mushrooms, half of the Swiss cheese and Parmesan. Set aside. In sauce pan, sauté green pepper in butter until tender. Stir in flour until thoroughly combined. Add milk, cook, stirring constantly until thickened and bubbly. Mix quarter of the sauce into ham mixture. Stuff shells with about ⅓ cup of filling in each shell. Place in greased 11x7 baking dish. Top with remaining sauce, sprinkle with paprika. Cover and bake at 350 degrees for 30 minutes. Sprinkle with remaining Swiss cheese and parsley.

HAMBURGER STROGANOFF
Pat Rhone

½ cup minced onion
¼ cup butter
1 tsp. salt
(8-oz.) can mushrooms
1 cup sour cream

1 clove garlic, minced
1 lb. ground beef
¼ tsp. pepper
1 can cream of chicken soup
1 pkg. noodles of choice

Sauté onion and garlic in butter for 5 minutes. Add meat and brown. Stir in salt, pepper, and mushrooms. Cook for 5 minutes. Add soup and simmer uncovered for 10 minutes. Stir in sour cream and heat through. Serve with noodles. Sprinkle with paprika.

HAMBURGER, POTATO AND PEAS CASSEROLE
Karen Churchill

1 lb. hamburger
onions, chopped (to taste)

4-5 potatoes
1 can peas

Brown hamburger with onions. Drain grease off well. Slice thinly and peel potatoes. Layer into a 1½ quart, round, covered casserole. Start and end with meat. Put sliced potatoes between each meat layer. Salt and pepper as desired. Bake at 350 degrees for 45 minutes. Then pour over peas - undrained. Bake another 10 minutes. Serves 4-6.

Recipe Note: You can double or triple for a larger family. You can use any vegetable (canned) but we prefer the green peas.

HOT HAM & CHEESE SANDWICHES

Sherry R. Letzelter

1/4 cup margarine, softened
2 T. horseradish mustard
2 T. finely chopped onion
2 tsp. poppy seeds (optional)

4 hamburger buns, split
8 slices thin, cooked ham
4 slices Swiss cheese

In bowl, combine the butter, mustard, onion, and poppy seeds. Spread on cut sides of buns. Layer ham and cheese on bottom halves, replace tops. Wrap each in foil, place on baking sheet. Bake at 350 degrees for 25 minutes (or until cheese is melted).

Recipe Note: This recipe is a great way to use up leftover ham.

ITALIAN CHICKEN

Donna Strong

1 envelope Good Seasons dressing
1/2 cup Parmesan cheese, grated

1/2 tsp. garlic powder
6 boneless chicken breasts, halved

Mix cheese, seasoning and garlic powder. Coat chicken in mixture. Place in 8x11 baking dish and bake at 350 degrees for 50-60 minutes.

ITALIAN CHICKEN STEW

Theresa Mahoney
Contributed by Rhonda Schember

6 boneless chicken breast halves,
  cut in bite-size pieces
1-2 cloves garlic, peeled
2 T. olive oil or canola oil
2 (15-oz.) cans tomato sauce
2 tsp. garlic salt

2 tsp. Italian seasonings
1 bay leaf
3 large potatoes, cut in bite-size
  pieces
1 (15-oz.) can cut green beans,
  drained

Sauté chicken pieces in hot oil with garlic until white. Add tomato sauce, seasonings and potatoes. Cook (simmer) over medium-low heat for 1 hour, covered. Add green beans 10 minutes before stew is done cooking. Adjust seasoning as needed.

74987-06

ITALIAN STUFFED PEPPERS

Olivia Balczon

8 green peepers
1-1½ lbs. hamburger
2 cloves garlic
3 T. parsley

4 slices white bread (wet with water and tear apart)
2 eggs (salt and pepper to taste)

Heat oven to 350 degrees. Place peppers in pot of water and boil until peppers soften, then drain. After stuffing the peppers, place in a greased pan and pout spaghetti sauce over all. Bake for 1 hour and sprinkle with grated cheese or put shredded mozzarella cheese over tops of stuffed peppers during the last 5 minutes of baking.

KID-FRIENDLY TUNA ROLL-UPS

Judy Lohse

DOUGH

1 cup Bisquick baking mix   ⅓ cup milk

Mix and roll out to approximate 6x12-inch long size pieces.

FILLING

1 small can tuna, drained   1 egg
2 T. minced onion

Mix and spread over and down the center of the dough. Fold up sides. Bake 350 degrees on cookie sheet until lightly browned, approximately 45 minutes. (Optional: Cutting 1-inch slices before folding up the sides can be alternately folded on the top to create a braided effect.) Slice and serve with cheese sauce, cheese soup or mushroom soup, slightly diluted. Can use an egg wash on top to give a shinier appearance.

CHEESE SAUCE

1 T. margarine
1 T. flour
1 cup milk

1 slice processed cheese (Velveeta) or Cheez Whiz to taste

In a saucepan, melt the ingredients.

Recipe Note: A Saturday lunch favorite with a salad. Serves 4.

MARZETTI

Debra Hull

Erie
Times-News

(8-oz.) grated sharp cheddar
  cheese
2 T. Crisco
1 lb. ground beef
½ green pepper, chopped
1 large onion, chopped
oregano
salt
pepper

garlic salt
sugar
dash Tabasco
(8-oz.) mushrooms
⅓ cup water
(6-oz.) tomato paste
(8-oz.) spaghetti
1 T. Worcestershire sauce

Grease a 9x12 pan. Make a meat mixture of all ingredients excluding cheese and spaghetti. Cook spaghetti. Make layers: spaghetti, meat mixture, cheese, and repeat until all ingredients are used. Top with cheese. Bake at 375 degrees for 20 minutes.

MEAT & POTATOES PIZZA

Jacque Mulson

1 lb. potatoes (about 3 medium)
1 (10-oz.) pkg. refrigerated,
  prepared pizza dough
½ lb. lean ground beef
2 cloves garlic, minced
salt and pepper to taste
1 cup prepared pizza or spaghetti
  sauce

1 sm. green or red bell pepper, cut
  into ¼-inch strips
1 (4-oz.) shredded part-skim
  mozzarella cheese
1 T. grated Parmesan cheese
¼ - ½ tsp. red pepper flakes

Slice potatoes ¼-inch thick; place in microwave-safe bowl with 2 cups water. Cover tightly. Microboil on HIGH for 15 minutes; drain, cool and set aside. Press dough into greased 12-inch round pizza pan; prick with fork. Bake in 425 degree oven for 10 minutes; set aside. Sauté beef and garlic in a skillet until brown. Salt and pepper to taste. To assemble pizza, spread ½ cup sauce on crust; top with potatoes, bell pepper and beef. Drizzle with remaining ½ cup sauce. Sprinkle with cheeses and pepper flakes. Bake 10-12 minutes or until hot and bubbly. Sprinkle with basil. Cut into 8 wedges; serve immediately. Makes 4 servings, 2 slices per serving.

74987-06

MEAT LASAGNA

Leslie Guelcher

SAUCE

1 lb. ground beef
1 lb. Italian sausage
1 large green pepper, diced
1 hot yellow pepper, diced
1 large onion, diced
3 cloves garlic, diced

1 (8-oz.) can tomato paste
4 fresh tomatoes, diced
1 T. fresh oregano
1 T. fresh basil
1 T. fresh parsley

FOR SAUCE: Start brown ground beef and Italian sausage in large, heavy saucepan over medium heat. Once meats are starting to brown, add peppers, onion and garlic. Sauté until the meat is browned. Add tomato paste and fresh tomatoes and herbs. Cover and simmer until flavors blend, stirring occasionally, about 15 minutes. Cool slightly.

CHEESE

2 (15-oz.) ctn. part-skim ricotta
   cheese
1 cup grated Parmesan cheese

2 large eggs, lightly whisked
4¾ cups grated mozzarella cheese

Combine ricotta and ¾ cup Parmesan cheese in medium bowl. Stir in two eggs. Blend completely.

ASSEMBLY

15 lasagna noodles
boiling water

salt

Preheat over to 350°F. Cook noodles in large pot of boiling salted water until almost tender, about 7 minutes. Drain and cover with cold water to stop cooking. ASSEMBLY: Drain pasta and pat dry. Spread ½ cup of sauce over bottom of 13x9-inch glass baking dish. Place 5 noodles over the sauce, overlapping to fit. Spread half of ricotta mixture evenly over noodles. Sprinkle with 2 cups mozzarella cheese evenly over ricotta. Spoon 1½ cups sauce over cheese, spreading with spatula to cover (sauce will be thick). Repeat layering with 5 noodles, remaining ricotta mixture, 2 cups mozzarella and 1½ cups sauce. Arrange remaining 5 noodles over sauce. Spread remaining sauce over noodles. Sprinkle remaining ¾ cup mozzarella cheese and ¼ cup Parmesan cheese evenly over lasagna. Can be prepared to this point 1 day ahead. Cover tightly with plastic wrap and refrigerate. Cover baking dish with aluminum foil. Bake lasagna 40 minutes; uncover and bake until hot and bubbly, about 40 minutes. Let lasagna stand 15 minutes before serving.

Recipe Note: This is a very versatile recipe. You can add vegetables, remove meat, or even change up the cheeses. I love the fresh ingredients in this recipe as it retains a lot of natural flavors.

MEATBALLS & GRAVY

Mary Ann Yonko

Erie
Times-News

1½ lbs. ground beef
1 lg. egg
1 med. onion, grated
½ cup seasoned bread crumbs
1 T. Worcestershire sauce

⅓ cup milk
salt, pepper, and parsley flakes
2 stalks celery, finely chopped
1 lg. carrot, chopped

Mix & shape into medium sized meatballs. Roll each one in flour. Brown in little oil in electric skillet. Add celery and carrot. Cover with water and simmer for about 1 hour. Add water as needed. Make gravy with flour and water and kitchen bouquet. Serve with rice, noodles or mashed potatoes.

MEXICAN CHICKEN
(Crock Pot recipe)

Lisa Shade

4 boneless, skinless chicken
  breasts
1 can black beans, rinsed and
  drained
1 can Del Monte zesty diced
  tomatoes with green chilies

1 jar roasted red reppers, chopped
1 med. onion, chopped
1 tsp. cumin

Rinse chicken and place in single layer at the bottom of a large crockery slow cooker (oval shape works best for four chicken breasts). In a separate bowl, combine remaining ingredients. Pour over chicken. DO NOT STIR. Cook on low 8-9 hours. Serve with white or brown rice and shredded cheddar cheese.

Recipe Note: Great leftovers! Shred chicken and combine well with bean and tomato mixture. Reheat, spoon into warm tortillas. Serve with shredded cheese, chunky salsa and low-fat sour cream.

74987-06

MEXICAN LASAGNA

Linda Heck

1 lb. ground beef
1 (16-oz.) can refried beans
2 tsp. dried oregano
1½ tsp. ground cumin
½ tsp. garlic powder
12 uncooked lasagna noodles
2½ cups water

2½ cups salsa
2 cups sour cream
¾ cup sliced green onions
1 (2-oz.) can sliced black olives
1 cup shredded Monterey Jack
  cheese

Brown ground beef in a skillet, combine beans, oregano, cumin and garlic powder. Using a 9x13 pan, place four uncooked noodles on the bottom of the pan. Spread half of the beef mixture over top of the noodles. Top with four more noodles, then add the rest of the beef mixture. Add four noodles to the top of the dish. Combine the salsa and water, then pour over all. Cover with foil, and bake for 1-1½ hours at 350 degrees. Stir the sour cream, black olives and green onions together. Then spoon over top of the casserole when finished baking and top with cheese. Place it back in the oven uncovered, until the cheese is melted.

NO FUSS BBQ RIBS

Dawn Blackburn

2 T. paprika
1 T. sugar
2 tsp. salt
2 tsp. chili powder
1½ tsp. black pepper
1 tsp. cumin

¼ tsp. red pepper
2 slabs of baby back ribs
1 foil cooking bag
1 cup approx. of your favorite
  BBQ sauce

Mix together all the dry ingredients and rub down the ribs well. Wrap and refrigerate for at least two hours or up to overnight. Place the racks into a foil bag with three ice cubes and seal. Grill over medium for about an hour turning only once. When ribs are fall-from-the-bone tender, remove from the bag and continue to grill 10 to 15 minutes longer basting with BBQ sauce.

NORTHERN FRIED CHICKEN

Ann Carson

1 cup pancake mix (Bisquick works well too)
2 to 3 tsp. salt
¼ tsp. fresh ground pepper

paprika
1 3- to 4-pound broiler/fryer chicken, cut up
oil (peanut) for deep-fat frying

In a large resealable plastic bag, combine the pancake mix, salt, pepper and paprika. Add the chicken, a few pieces at a time; shake to coat. Heat 2 inches of oil in an electric skillet or deep-fat fryer to 375 degrees. Fry the chicken, a few pieces at a time for 6 minutes; turn and cook 6 minutes longer or until golden brown and juices run clear. Yield: 4 to 6 servings.

Recipe Note:

Note: I use a candy thermometer to check the temperature.

ORIENTAL CORNISH HENS

Sandy Reid

CORNISH HENS

4 (16-oz.) Cornish hens, thawed and cleaned
⅓ cup chopped Vidalia onion
⅓ cup chopped celery
2 T. butter or margarine for frying
1 cup uncooked regular rice

1 (14-oz.) can chicken broth; may use good bouillon
1 (8-oz.) can crushed pineapple in juice, drained
2 T. butter or margarine for basting

Thaw hens if frozen. Heat oven to 350 degrees. Wash hens and pat dry. In a medium skillet, cook and stir onion and celery in 2 tablespoons butter until onion is tender. Stir in rice and chicken broth. Heat to boiling, stirring occasionally. Heat to boiling, stirring occasionally. Reduce heat; cover tightly and simmer over low heat about 20 minutes or until all of the liquid is absorbed. Stir in pineapple. Stuff hens lightly with rice mixture; fasten openings with skewers or toothpicks. Place hens breast side up on a rack in an open shallow roasting pan. Brush with melted butter. Do not add water. Do not cover. Roast for 90 minutes brushing with butter or pan drippings.

SAUCE

⅓ cup sugar
1 tsp. cornstarch
⅓ cup regular or low sodium soy sauce

¼ tsp. ground ginger

While hens roast, stir together sugar and cornstarch in a small saucepan. Stir in soy sauce and ginger. If you prefer, you may use a small amount of fresh minced ginger root in place of the ground ginger. Cook over medium heat, stirring constantly until mixture thickens and boils. Boil and stir 1 minute. Cool. Brush hens with soy mixture. Place hens on a warmed platter or individual plates; pour remaining sauce over hens or serve separately.

Recipe Note: These hens can be served hot or cold. I have taken them to picnics and fancy Sunday dinner and they are always a hit. This recipe can be changed slightly by adding fresh chopped peaches instead of the pineapple. Feel free to add some minced ginger root to the stuffing as well.

OVERNIGHT TUNA CASSEROLE

Sherry R. Letzelter

I can cream of celery soup,
  undiluted
I cup milk
I (6-oz.) can tuna, drained

I cup uncooked elbow macaroni
I cup frozen peas
I cup shredded cheddar cheese,
  divided

In a bowl, combine soup and milk until smooth. Add the tuna, macaroni, peas, and ¾ cup cheese; mix well. Pour into a greased 2-quart dish. Cover and refrigerate overnight. Microwave, covered, on high for 14 to 16 minutes, or until bubbly. Uncover, sprinkle with remaining cheese and let stand for 5 minutes. Serves 4.

Recipe Note: Quick and easy. My family requests this meal often.

PARMESAN CHICKEN

Jennie Geisler
From the Erie Times–News

¼ cup grated Parmesan cheese
¼ cup Italian seasoned bread
  crumbs

½ tsp. paprika
4 (4-oz.) boneless, skinless chicken
  breasts

Preheat oven to 400 degrees. Spray a baking sheet with cooking spray. Blend cheese, crumbs and paprika in a plastic zip-top baggie. Pour into a shallow bowl or plate and coat chicken breasts. Arrange chicken breasts on the baking sheet and bake 30 minutes, or until juices run clear.

Recipe Note: This was originally a Weight Watchers recipe, but I altered the mixture because I like more cheese than bread crumbs. This is what I fix when I can't think of anything else, because it's so easy it's practically mindless. Goes great with a side of rotini and tomato sauce.

74987-06

PASTA WITH MUSSELS
(Fast and Easy)

Leslie Guelcher

1 pkg. mussels from Wegmans or Giant Eagle
1 large green pepper, diced
1 large yellow pepper, diced
1 large red pepper, diced
1 small hot pepper, diced
1 large yellow onion, diced
4 cloves garlic, diced
1 tsp. fresh thyme
1 cup dry white wine
2 cups low-sodium chicken broth
1 cup grated Parmesan cheese
12 oz. angel hair pasta

MUSSELS: Fill a sink with COLD water to clean the mussels. Fill a large bowl with cold water. You want to keep them cold so they do not open before cooking. Place the mussels in the sink. Scrub the shell to remove dirt. Pull off the "beard" on the outside of the shell. Transfer the mussel to the bowl. Continue process until all mussels have been cleaned. COOKING: In a large saucepan, heat the oil over high heat. Add the peppers, onion, garlic and thyme, sauté briefly, about 3 minutes. Add the white wine and chicken broth, bring to a boil. Drain the mussels and add them to the broth mixture. Mix the mussels into the mixture. Cover and steam for 6-7 minutes, until the mussels open. Remove pot from heat, remove all un-opened mussels, cover and set aside. PASTA: In a separate saucepan, bring 10 cups of water to a boil. Add pasta; cook until tender but still firm, stirring occasionally. Drain. SERVE: Serve in a large dish. Set pasta in the dish, spoon the mussels and broth mixture over the pasta. Sprinkle Parmesan cheese on the top and serve the remaining Parmesan on the side.

Recipe Note: A warm loaf of French bread is a great accompaniment for this recipe.

PASTA WITH PUMPKIN AND SAUSAGE

Jennie Geisler
From the Erie Times–News

Erie Times-News

2 T. olive oil
1 lb. hot Italian turkey sausage, casings removed
1 medium onion, chopped
10 cloves garlic, chopped
3 T. chopped fresh sage
1¼ cups white wine
1¼ cups canned pumpkin purée
2 cups fat-free, low-sodium chicken broth
¼ tsp. cinnamon
salt and pepper to taste
1 T. salt
1 lb. penne, penne rigate, rigatoni or tortiglioni
6 T. freshly grated Parmesan

In a large, deep sauté pan, heat 1 tablespoon of olive oil. Add the sausage and cook until brown, about 3 minutes. While it browns, break it up into bite-sized pieces with the back of a wooden spoon. Turn off heat and remove the sausage to a bowl with a slotted spoon. Move to a plate covered with paper towels to drain. Keep 1 tablespoon of the oil left in the pan, and discard the rest. Add the remaining 2 tablespoons olive oil and heat well. Add the onion, garlic and sage and cook 10 minutes, stirring well, until the onion and garlic start to brown. Add the sausage and cook 2 minutes, stirring well. Deglaze the pan with the wine and cook 8 minutes, stirring well to dislodge any browned bits from the bottom of the pan. Add the pumpkin purée and cook 2 minutes, stirring well. Add the stock, bring to a boil over high heat, then reduce heat and simmer 30 minutes. Add cinnamon, salt and pepper to taste in the last 5 minutes. While the sauce is simmering, bring a large pot of water to boil, with 1 tablespoon of salt added, to a boil over high heat. Add the pasta and cook to al dente. Drain well in a colander and pour into the sauce and cook over medium heat for 3 minutes, stirring constantly Remove from heat, add the Parmesan and serve. Makes 8 2-cup servings.

Recipe Note: This is one of the most intriguing recipes I can remember trying. I never would have if food editor Jeff Hileman hadn't raved about it in the office one day. I'm so very glad he did. This is adapted from www.nickstellino.com. Per servings: 395 calories, 10 grams of fat and 4 grams fiber.

74987-06

PHILLY BURGERS

Holly Fleger

1 lb. lean ground beef
1 (3-oz.) pkg. cream cheese,
  softened
1 can French-fried onions
3 T. Dijon mustard

2 T. Worcestershire sauce
1 (4-oz.) can sliced mushrooms,
  drained
4 hamburger buns

In mixing bowl combine ground beef, ½ cup of fried onions, 1 T. mustard, 1 T. Worcestershire sauce. Mix well. Form into 4 patties and place in broiler. Broil for about 6 minutes, flip and broil for about 6 more minutes. While burgers are cooking, mix cream cheese, 2 T. mustard, and 1 T. Worcestershire sauce until creamy. Mix in mushrooms. Once burgers have cooked on both sides, top each with the cream cheese mix, then sprinkle French fried onions on each one. Broil for 30 seconds more. Remove from broiler and serve on buns.

Recipe Note: Once you top the burgers with the cream cheese mixture and onions, don't cook longer than 30 seconds. The French-fried onions burn very easily.

PIZZA CASSEROLE

Caroline Mulson

1½ lbs. ground beef
1 med. green pepper, chopped
1 (29-oz.) can spaghetti sauce
1 (16-oz.) can pizza sauce
1 (16-oz.) pkg. wide noodles,
  cooked and drained

1 (8-oz.) pkg. pepperoni sliced
1 (12-oz.) pkg. shredded mozzarella
  cheese
1 sm. onion, chopped

Brown ground beef, green pepper and onion in frying pan on the stove; drain well. Add spaghetti and pizza sauces. Placed cooked noodles in bottom of 9x13 baking dish. Place meat sauce over top. Lay pepperoni slices on sauce, sprinkle cheese over top. Cover; bake at 350 degrees for 35 minutes or until cheese is bubbly.

Recipe Note: A great side dish to take to a family picnic or holiday event.

PIZZA CHICKEN ROLL-UPS

Sherry R. Letzelter

4 boneless chicken breast halves   8 slices mozzarella cheese, divided
12 slices pepperoni   1 (15-oz.) can pizza sauce

Flatten chicken to ¼-inch thickness. Place 3 slices of pepperoni and 1 slice of cheese on each. Roll up tightly and secure with toothpicks. Place in a greased baking pan. Spoon pizza sauce over roll-ups. Cover and bake at 350 degrees for 35 to 40 minutes. Uncover, top with remaining cheese. Bake 5 - 10 minutes longer or until cheese is melted.

Recipe Note: This recipe is both simple to make and delicious!

PIZZA CORDON "BLUE"

Jacque Mulson

½ sm. onion   ¼ cup reduced-fat sour cream
1½ cup sliced, fresh mushrooms   ¾ cup cooked chicken chunks
½ green pepper, chopped   ¾ cup deli ham chunks
1 partially baked pizza crust   1 cup shredded Swiss cheese
2 T. Dijon mustard

Heat oven to 450 degrees. Peel and thinly slice onion. Place slices in microwave-safe dish. Add mushrooms and peppers. Microwave on high until onion and peppers are wilted and mushrooms have released their liquid, about 2-3 minutes. Place pizza crust on ungreased baking sheet while vegetables cook. Stir together mustard and sour cream, and spread evenly over crust. Cut chicken and ham pieces so they're bite-size; sprinkle evenly over crust. Drain liquid from cooked vegetables and distribute vegetables over pizza. Sprinkle cheese evenly on top. Bake until pizza begins to brown at edges and cheese melts, 10-12 minutes. Serves 4-8.

Recipe Note: A different, but delicious idea for a pizza!

PORK CHOPS

Nancy Group

6 pork chops   1 cup ketchup
1 cup applesauce

Brown pork chops. Mix applesauce and ketchup in large crock pot. Add pork chops. Cook on high for about 5 hours or until pork chops are very tender. May also be done in a large pot on the stove, for about 3 or 4 hours using medium heat. Recipe can easily be adjusted for more pork chops.

74987-06

PORK TENDERLOIN WITH MUSTARD SAUCE
Karen Oliver

¼ cup soy sauce
¼ cup bourbon

2 T. brown sugar
2 1-lb. pork tenderloins

Combine first 3 ingredients in a 9x13 pan. Add tenderloins. Cover and refrigerate at least 4 hours turning meat occasionally. Remove from marinade; place on a rack in a shallow roasting pan. Bake at 325 degrees for 45 minutes. Serve with mustard sauce.

MUSTARD SAUCE

⅔ cup sour cream
⅔ cup mayonnaise
2 T. dry mustard

3 to 4 green onions, finely
  chopped

Combine sour cream, mayonnaise, dry mustard and green onions. Cover and chill.

PORK TENDERLOIN WITH ROASTED POTATOES
Karen Oliver

2 1-lb. pork tenderloins
½ cup olive oil
1 T. dried rosemary
1 tsp. dried thyme

3 cloves of garlic minced
1 tsp. salt and pepper
2 lbs. new red potatoes, cut in
  half

Combine olive oil, rosemary, thyme, garlic salt and pepper in a zipper-top bag. Take out about ¼ cup of the mixture and set aside. Place pork tenderloins in the bag and coat. Marinate overnight. When ready to cook meat, coat the potatoes with the remaining marinade mixture. Preheat oven to 375 degrees. Place tenderloins and potatoes in a 9x13 baking pan. Bake for 45-50 minutes.

PUMPKIN CHILI
Jennie Geisler
From the Erie Times–News

2 lb. lean ground beef
1 large onion
1 medium green bell pepper, diced
2 (15-19-oz.) cans red kidney
  beans, drained
1 (46-oz.) can tomato juice

1 (26-28 oz.) can peeled and diced
  tomatoes with juice
½ cup canned pumpkin purée
1 T. pumpkin pie spice
1 T. chili powder
¼ cup sugar

In a large pot over medium heat, cook beef until brown, drain. Stir in onion and bell pepper and cook 5 minutes. Stir in beans, tomato juice, diced tomatoes and pumpkin purée. Season with pumpkin pie spice, chili powder and sugar. Simmer 1 hour. Makes 16-20 cups.

Recipe Note: This recipe will warm you to your toes, especially after a long day of holiday preparations. Per cup: 184 calories, 2.5 grams fat, 3.1 grams fiber, 13.9 grams carbohydrate, 143.2 grams sodium.

REUBEN BAKE

Melissa Lesniewski

5 cups peeled, cubed baking potato
⅓ cup fat-free sour cream
¼ cup skim milk
½ tsp. salt
¼ tsp. pepper
cooking spray
4 cups packaged angel hair slaw

1 cup finely chopped lean deli corned beef (about ¼ lb)
½ tsp. caraway seeds
¼ cup fat-free or low-fat Thousand Island dressing
1¼ cups shredded Swiss cheese, divided (5 oz.)
paprika

Preheat oven to 350 degrees. Place potato in saucepan; cover with water, and bring to a boil. Cover, reduce heat, and simmer 20 minutes or until very tender; drain well. Combine potato, sour cream, and next 3 ingredients; beat at medium speed of a mixer for 2 minutes or until smooth. Set aside. Coat a nonstick skillet with cooking spray; place over medium heat until hot. Add cabbage, corned beef, and caraway seeds; sauté 4 minutes or until cabbage wilts. Remove from heat; stir in dressing. Spread half of potato mixture in bottom of an 11x7 baking dish coated with cooking spray; top with cabbage mixture, and sprinkle with 1 cup cheese. Spread remaining potato mixture over cheese; top with remaining ¼ cup cheese, and sprinkle with paprika. Bake at 350 degrees for 40 minutes or until golden. Yield: 6 servings (serving size 1⅓ cups)

Recipe Note: Recipe is adapted from Weight Watchers Six O' Clock Solutions Cookbook.

SALISBURY STEAK

Kathleen Dahl

1½ lb. ground beef
½ cup milk
½ pkg. onion soup mix
¾ cup seasoned bread crumbs
3 cups mushroom soup

1 egg
dash pepper
flour
shortening

Combine beef, egg, milk, onion soup mix, bread crumbs, and pepper. Form into patties. Roll in flour and brown in shortening. Place in baking dish and cover with mushroom soup. Bake at 350 degrees for 45 minutes.

74987-06

SAUCY CHICKEN CASSEROLE
Pearl Schwindt

I can cream of chicken soup
I can cream of mushroom soup
2 cups sour cream
¾ cup chicken broth
½ medium onion, chopped
I cup fresh mushrooms, sliced
½ tsp. garlic powder

½ tsp. salt
½ tsp. poultry seasoning
¼ tsp. black pepper
6 boneless, chicken breast halves
cooked noodles or rice
chopped parsley

In 13x9 baking pan combine soups, sour cream, broth, mushrooms, onion and seasonings. Arrange chicken on top of sauce. Bake uncovered at 350 degrees for 1 hour or until chicken is tender. Serve chicken and sauce over noodles or rice of your choice. Garnish with parsley. Serves 6.

SAUSAGE AND RICE CASSEROLE
Linda Heck

I lb. bulk Italian sausage
I cup celery
½ cup chopped onion
¼ cup sweet red pepper
¼ cup green pepper
½ cup sliced fresh mushrooms

I (8-oz.) can sliced water chestnuts
I cup uncooked long-grain rice
2 cups chicken broth
½ tsp. salt
½ tsp. pepper
½ tsp. sage

Brown sausage in a skillet over medium heat, place sausage in a 2½ quart casserole dish. In the grease from the sausage, sauté the celery, onion, red peppers, green peppers and mushrooms until they are no longer crisp. Put on top of the sausage in the casserole dish. Add water chestnuts, rice, broth, and salt and pepper to the casserole dish, and mix well. Cover and bake for 60-75 minutes at 350 degrees.

74987-06

SAVORY CHICKEN VEGETABLE STRUDEL
Ramona Piazza

Erie
Times-News

2 cups diced, cooked chicken
½ cup shredded carrots
½ cup finely chopped broccoli
⅓ cup finely chopped sweet red pepper
1 (4-oz.) shredded sharp cheddar cheese
½ cup mayonnaise
2 cloves garlic, minced
½ tsp. dill weed
¼ tsp. salt
¼ tsp. pepper
2 (8-oz.) tubes refrigerated crescent rolls
1 egg white, beaten
2 T. slivered almonds

In a bowl, combine the first 10 ingredients; mix well. Unroll crescent dough and place in a greased 15x10x1 baking pan; press seams and perforations together, forming a 15x12 rectangle (dough will hang over edge of pan). Spread filling lengthwise down the center of dough. On each long side, cut 1½" wide strips 3½" into center. Starting at one end, alternate strips, twisting twice and laying at an angle across filling. Seal ends. Brush dough with egg whites; sprinkle with almonds. Bake at 375 degrees for 30-35 minutes or until golden brown. Cut into slices; serve warm. Yields 12 servings.

SAVORY LEFTOVER CRESCENT SQUARES
Barbara Valaitis

1 (3-oz.) pkg. cream cheese, softened (regular or fat-free)
3 T. butter, melted
3 cups cooked, cubed chicken, beef, or turkey
¼ tsp. salt
⅛ tsp. pepper
2 T. milk, skim, regular or non-fat
1 T. onion or chive, chopped
1 T. pimento, chopped (optional)
1 (8-oz.) can crescent rolls
¾ cup croutons seasoned, crushed

Preheat oven to 350 degrees. Blend cream cheese and 2 tablespoons of melted butter, (reserve 1 tablespoon of melted butter), until smooth. Add meat, salt, pepper, milk, onion/chives, and pimento. Mix well. Separate dough into 4 rectangles; press firmly along the perforations to seal. Spoon ½ cup of meat mixture into center of each rectangle. Pull the 4 corners towards the center of each rectangle, twisting slightly and sealing edges. Brush the tops with reserved melted butter and dip into crushed bread crumbs. Bake on ungreased cookie sheet for about 20-25 minutes or until golden brown. Refrigerate any leftovers. Serves 4.

74987-06

SCALLOPS WITH PASTA & SPINACH

Jade Conners

2 T. oil
1 cup slivered sweet red peppers
2 T. minced garlic
1/8 to 1/4 tsp. cayenne pepper
1/2 cups finely chopped onion
1/3 cup lemon juice
1 T. brown sugar
1 T. minced lemon zest
1 tsp. salt

1 tsp. black pepper
3/4 lb. spaghetti, linguine, penne, curly pasta or curly noodles
5 cups clean, shredded loosely packed spinach or 1, 10 oz. pkg. frozen, thawed
1 to 1 1/2 lbs. cleaned scallops
1/3 cup coarsely chopped feta cheese (optional)

Heat oil in 12-inch heavy skillet on med-low heat until hot; add peppers, garlic and cayenne. Cook 5 minutes. Add onions and cook, uncovered, until vegetables are tender, stirring, 8-10 minutes. Add scallops and cook until done. Add lemon juice, sugar, zest, salt and pepper; heat 1 minute. Cook pasta according to package. About 1 minute before pasta is cooked, add spinach. Drain and place in large, warm serving bowl; add sauce and toss to coat. Sprinkle cooked and warmed scallops over pasta and toss with feta cheese.

SEAFOOD LASAGNA

Stacy Wing

1 cup chopped onion, sautéed
2 T. butter
1 (8-oz.) pkg. softened cream cheese
1 1/2 cups cottage cheese
1 egg
2 tsp. dried basil
1/4 tsp. pepper and salt
1/2 cup grated Parmesan cheese

1 can cream of shrimp soup or shrimp bisque
1/2 can milk
1/3 cup white wine
1/3 cup milk
1 lb. chopped cooked shrimp
1 (8-oz.) pkg. crab meat (real or imitation)
1 box lasagna noodles, uncooked

Mix first 8 ingredients. This is your cheese mixture. Mix the next 6 ingredients together in a separate bowl. This is your seafood mixture. DO NOT cook the noodles. Place one layer of noodles in a greased 8x11.5x2 casserole dish. Spread half of the cheese mixture over noodles, then spread half the seafood mixture over cheese. Repeat layers. Sprinkle with some Parmesan cheese. Cover casserole dish with foil and place on a baking sheet. Bake at 350 degrees for 45 minutes, then uncover and bake another 30 to 45 minutes until set. This recipe may be doubled and baked in a deep lasagna pan.

SEAFOOD PIZZA

Lisa Dietrich

Erie
Times-News

1 prebaked pizza shell
6 jumbo shrimp, cooked,
  chopped, tails removed
4 oz. crab meat, chopped
1½ cups shredded Italian-blend
  cheese
olive oil
1 tsp. minced garlic

1 tsp. dry Ranch dressing mix
salt
pepper
diced tomatoes (optional)
sliced olives (optional)
red/green/yellow peppers
  (optional)

Marinate shrimp and crabmeat in 1½ tablespoons olive oil, 1 teaspoon minced garlic, 1 teaspoon dry Ranch dressing mix and salt and pepper to taste, for 30 minutes. Brush pizza crust with olive oil. Sprinkle one cup of cheese over the crust. Top with shrimp and crab mixture. Add any additional desired toppings. Top with remaining cheese and sprinkle with pepper. Bake on a pizza pan in a 400-degree oven for 8-10 minutes until crust is golden brown and cheese is melted. Let rest for 5 minutes, cut and serve.

SOUTHERN PULLED PORK BARBECUE

Jane (Rohleder) Voltz

1 pork tenderloin
2 cups Kraft honey or spicy
  honey barbecue sauce
1 cup apple butter

½ to ¾ cup very finely chopped
  onions
10 to 12 fresh Kaiser rolls
coleslaw

Cook one whole pork tenderloin in a slow cooker on high for 5 to 6 hours. Season as you like. I usually add water and bullion, along with onions and celery while it cooks. Meanwhile, while the tenderloin is cooking, mix the honey barbeque sauce, apple butter, and finely chopped onions together. When the tenderloin is tender and falling apart, pull it, using 2 forks. Put the pulled pork into a pan. Mix the barbecue sauce with the pork. (Depending on the size of your tenderloin and how much sauce you like, you may not need to add all of the sauce. Add it according to your taste.) Heat in pan until warm. Serve on fresh rolls with homemade coleslaw.

Recipe Note: In the South, they put the coleslaw right on the sandwich, but as an Erieite, I still eat mine on the side. This is very simple, and the apple butter gives it a delightful, almost sweet taste. Enjoy!!!

74987-06

SOUTHERN STYLE BONELESS COUNTRY RIBS
Eileen Alberstadt

5 lbs. boneless pork ribs
garlic salt

paprika
barbecue sauce

Heat oven to 350 degrees. Wash the ribs in ice-cold water and pat dry. Place in large roaster or deep casserole dish. Sprinkle garlic salt and paprika to form a rub. Ribs should be placed next to each other and equally rubbed. Cover with foil (shiny side down). Place in oven for 1½ hours. Pull from oven and brush with barbeque sauce cover and place back in oven for an additional 40 minutes. Add additional barbecue sauce before serving if desired. These ribs should fall apart when they touch your fork.

Recipe Note: Best served with baked potatoes, a green vegetable and don't forget the tomato and cucumber salad.

SPAGHETTI SAUCE AND MEATBALLS
Jennie Geisler
From the Erie Times–News

1 (29-oz.) can tomato sauce
1 (14½ - oz.) can petite diced
  tomatoes
1 (5.9 oz.) can tomato paste
1 T. dried basil
1 T. dried oregano
¼ cup sugar
½ tsp. cumin or caraway seed
1 medium onion, chopped
1 clove garlic, minced
salt and pepper to taste

1 lb. 95 percent fat-free ground
  beef
1 large egg
1 T. dried basil
1 T. dried oregano
pepper to taste
1 medium onion, chopped
1 clove garlic
⅓ cup grated Parmesan cheese
2 T. fresh parsley, chopped
⅓ cup bread crumbs

Combine first 10 ingredients in slow cooker. Heat on low for 8 hours. When sauce is ready, prepare meatballs. Grease a cookie sheet and preheat oven to 400 degrees. Combine remaining ingredients, but don't work the mixture too much. Gently form into balls and bake approximately 20 minutes, or until brown. Add to sauce and serve.

Recipe Note: I got all kind of heck for this recipe, because the meatballs contain onions, if I remember correctly, but I decided to include it anyway, because it's so good. The beauty of these is that they're a lot lighter than regular meatballs, and pretty darned tasty, too. If the onion offends you, feel free to leave it out.

SPAGHETTI SOPHIA

Leo Swigonski

6 T. olive oil
6 cloves garlic
1 (16-oz.) can peeled tomatoes (any
  type)

¾ T. basil & oregano
1 tsp. sugar

Heat the olive oil. When warm, add the finely diced garlic, the can of tomatoes, basil, oregano and sugar. Simmer on Low for about 30 minutes, stirring whenever the thought strikes you. Now comes the absolute best component of Sophia's recipe! You can go free-style with any or all ingredients you may so wish to add. For me, I start with the above ingredients and add equal amount of finely diced onion and celery. We add red or green pepper and mushrooms whenever the spirit moves me. In a separate saucepan, sometimes we brown a patty or three of sweet Italian sausage or maybe just plain 'ol reliable ground chuck, draining off the fatty juices. Sometimes homemade meatballs and/or hunks of spicy Italian sausage make it to the basic sauce plan. We keep the extra fancy additives separate for those that do not like 'the works!' The fragrance is absolutely intoxicating! The pasta, about a box of your choice type, should be a boilin' and while it's simmerin' and stirrin' your 'Sophia' sauce, prepare a salad and slice a loaf of Tuscan Italian bread if you wish. When ready to serve your pasta feast, top with Romano or Parmesan cheese or go nuts with both!

Recipe Note: Every time we prepare this, it is different in ingredient make-up so the desire for it never leaves. As Mayberry Andy Griffith used to compliment 'ol Aunt Bea, "Hhmm-hhmm good!!!" (If Sophia Loren ever makes town, I'll put her up for a good feed ... count on it!)

74987-06

STUFFED CHILES RELLENOS
(Mexican Stuffed Peppers)

Maggie Wilson

4 poblano peppers, roasted with seeds and skin removed (see directions below)
1 lb. hamburger
1 clove garlic, finely minced
1 sm. onion, diced
1 (10-oz.) can Old El Paso enchilada sauce, medium or mild depending on desired heat
1 to 1½ cups cheddar or Monterey Jack cheese, grated
1 T. olive oil
cooking spray
salsa (optional)
sour cream (optional)

To roast poblano peppers, place peppers directly on a stovetop gas flame turned up high. Alternately, peppers may be placed on an outdoor gas or charcoal grill. Roasting peppers inside may get a bit smoky. Turn peppers until all outside skin is blackened and blistered, about 10 minutes. Place peppers in a plastic food storage bag and seal for about 10 minutes. Remove peppers and gently scrape blackened outside skin off and discard skin. Cut off stems and remove seeds inside the pepper. If you like it hot and spicy, leave the seeds inside. Preheat oven to 375 degrees. In a medium sauté pan, heat olive oil and break up hamburger. Add in garlic and cook until meat is no longer pink. Add can of enchilada sauce, cook two minutes or until hot. Remove from heat. Coat an 8x8 or 9x13 casserole dish with cooking spray. Using a small spoon, gently stuff each pepper with hamburger mixture and cheese until full. Place in casserole dish and use remaining cheese and hamburger mixture to spread on top of peppers. Bake at 375 degrees for 20 minutes or until hot. Serve with sour cream and salsa, if desired. Wrap inside soft tortillas or top tortilla chips or serve with hot cooked rice.

SUNDAY GRAVY

Stephanie Reid

My favorite Italian dish that my
Polish Mom makes!

¼ cup extra virgin olive oil plus 3 tablespoons

7 cloves garlic, peeled and sliced thin

pinch crushed red pepper flakes

6 (6-oz.) cans tomato paste

2 sprig fresh oregano

1 tsp. salt

9 whole fresh basil leaves

12 (6-oz.) cans water

3 No. 2 can whole tomatoes, with juice, puréed (35-oz.)

1½ No. 2 can tomato cans of water

1 recipe polpetti (meatballs)

1 recipe bracciole di maiale (stuffed pork roll)

¾ lb. beef stew meat cut into large cubes

1 lb. Italian sausage, sweet or hot

Place the ¼ cup of olive oil in a very large heavy-bottomed sauce pot over medium heat. Sauté the garlic for about 1 minute or until it is slightly golden. Add the tomato paste and fry it with the garlic for 5 minutes or until the paste is bubbling, constantly stirring so as not to burn it. Stir in the 12 tomato paste cans of water and allow to simmer for 20 minutes or until thick. This is always the way we measured water at our house for sauce. Good way to clean the cans, too. Add the puréed tomatoes, the 1½ tomato cans of water, the oregano, salt, basil and red pepper flakes. Bring to a boil then lower the heat so that the sauce barely simmers. Place a wooden spoon under the cover to keep the pot partially opened. While the sauce cooks, place the remaining olive oil in a large skillet over medium-high heat and begin to brown the meat components evenly on all sides. When browned, add meat to sauce and simmer until tender. Serve over your favorite pasta! Magna!

POLPETTI

3 T. extra virgin olive oil

1 small white onion, finely chopped

3 cloves garlic, finely chopped

2½ lbs. meat loaf mix

1¼ cups fresh bread crumbs

¾ cup Pecorino Romano cheese

12 sprig Italian parsley, chopped

salt and freshly ground pepper to taste

8 extra large eggs

Place 1 tablespoon of the olive oil in a skillet over medium heat. Sauté the onion and garlic in it for 3 minutes or until the onion is translucent. Set aside and allow to cool. In a large bowl, mix together the meat loaf mix, bread crumbs, cheese, the cooled onion and garlic, parsley, salt, pepper and eggs. Shape the mixture into medium sized ovals, the size of the extra large eggs. You should end up with about 22 meatballs. Brown the meatballs in 2 tablespoons of olive oil and proceed with the recipe for the famous "Sunday Gravy" or simply submerge them in your favorite tomato sauce and gently simmer until tender. If you are in a hurry, place all of the meatballs on a

(continued)

74987-06

cookie sheet that has been sprayed with cooking spray and bake for about 10 minutes at 350 degrees.

BRACCIOLE DI MAIALE/
STUFFED PORK ROLL

1 3-lb. boneless pork loin
salt and pepper to taste
2 cloves garlic, finely chopped
(8-oz.) mild provolone, cut to a
  medium dice
1 T. grated Parmesan cheese
1 small white onion, finely
  chopped
3 sprig Italian parsley, stems
  removed

4 whole basil leaves
2 sweet Italian sausages, casing
  removed and sautéed then
  chopped
1 hard-boiled egg, chopped
2 T. virgin olive oil
1 recipe for the famous "Sunday
  Gravy"

Cut a deep slit down the center of the center of the pork loin and open it so it lays flat. This procedure is known as "butterflying". Season the meat with salt and pepper to taste. Mix the garlic, provolone, Parmesan, onion, parsley, basil, chopped egg and the sautéed sausage well in a bowl. Lay the mixture evenly down the center of the meat. Roll the meat up tightly, tying it with butcher's twine at 1-inch intervals. Secure the ends with toothpicks if needed. Place the olive oil in a skillet over medium-high heat. Brown the pork roll all over then simmer it, submerged in the Sunday Gravy, over very low heat until tender, about 1 to 1½ hours. When the bracciole is done, remove it to a cutting board, cut off the twine, pull out and discard the toothpicks. Slice the bracciole into ½-inch thick slices, place on a warm platter and serve with sauce. The bracciole can also be roasted in the oven and topped with your favorite sauce.

Recipe Note: When I make this bracciole, the pork loin is always big enough for two, so I put one in the sauce and the other in the freezer. Its great to have on hand for a quick, elegant dinner in a snap! This Sunday Gravy Recipe was featured a few years ago in the Sunday Erie Times-News.

TACO BISCUIT CASSEROLE

Jeremiah Mulson

Erie
Times-News

1½ lbs. lean (at least 80%) ground beef
1 (1.25-oz.) pkg. taco seasoning mix
¾ cup water
1¼ cups salsa
1 (16.3-oz.) can homestyle or flaky refrigerated biscuits
2 cups shredded Mexican cheese blend

shredded lettuce
chopped tomatoes
additional salsa
sliced ripe olives, drained
sour cream
sliced green onions

Heat oven to 375 degrees. In a 10-inch skillet, brown beef over medium-high heat for 8-10 minutes, stirring frequently, until thoroughly cooked; drain. Stir in taco seasoning mix, water and salsa; heat to boiling. Reduce heat to low; simmer 3 minutes. Remove from heat. Separate dough into 8 biscuits. Cut each biscuit into 8 pieces. Add pieces to beef mixture; stir gently. Spoon mixture into ungreased 13x9 pan. Bake 18-20 minutes or until sauce is bubbly and biscuits are golden brown. Sprinkle with cheese. Bake an additional 8-10 minutes or until cheese is bubbly. To serve, cut into 8 squares. Top with remaining ingredients. Makes 8 servings.

Recipe Note: Fun and easy to make!

TANGY MUSTARD BASIL CHICKEN

Karen Oliver

¾ cup lowfat buttermilk
⅓ cup lowfat plain yogurt
¼ cup honey
2 tsp. dried basil

2 T. coarse ground Dijon mustard
⅛ tsp. black pepper
6 boneless, skinless chicken breasts

Combine buttermilk, yogurt, honey, mustard, basil and pepper in a plastic bag. Mix well. Place chicken in marinade coating both sides. Refrigerate several hours or overnight, turning bag occasionally. To grill: Remove chicken from marinade and cook about 7 minutes on each side.

Recipe Note: Chicken may be cooked in the oven if desired. Preheat oven to 375 degrees. Place chicken on a baking sheet. Coat with marinade. Bake 20-25 minutes or until juices run clear. Makes 6 servings.

74987-06

TATER TOT CASSEROLE
(Quick and Easy)

Elizabeth Korb

1 1-lb. cooked hamburger
1 (16-oz.) sour cream
1 (14-oz.) can cream of mushroom
  soup

1 (16-oz.) bag shredded cheddar
  cheese
1 bag frozen tater tots

Preheat oven to 350 degrees. Add cooked hamburger into a 9x13 glass pan. Add creamed soup (no water or milk added) and stir into the cooked hamburger, spread out in pan. Add a layer of shredded cheese, then sour cream. Last, add a layer of FROZEN tater tots on the top. Bake for 20-25 minutes, or until tater tots are a golden brown. Remove from oven and sprinkle with more shredded cheese. Ready to serve under 25 minutes!!!

TOFU BURGERS

Dawn Blackburn

1 lb. firm tofu
1 small shredded carrot
1 chopped small onion
1 tsp. Italian seasoning

2 T. parsley
½ tsp. garlic powder
¼ cup approx. flour
¼ cup vegetable oil

Mix all ingredients except flour together well. Add flour until mixture holds together. (You may need more depending on the water content of the tofu.) Form into serving sized patties. Mixture should hold its shape well without crumbling. Heat vegetable oil over medium temperature and fry patties for about 5 minutes or so on each side or until golden brown. Try to flip only once. Drain on paper towels and serve.

TOUCHDOWN SANDWICHES

Rosemarie Pitetti

1 (12-oz.) deli ham
1 cup shredded cheddar cheese
¼ cup drained sweet pickle relish

1 T. mustard
2 T. mayonnaise
8 hamburger buns

Cut ham into small cubes. Toss ham, cheese and relish lightly. Mix mayonnaise and mustard together. Stir into meat mixture. Divide evenly onto the hamburger buns. Wrap individually in foil. Bake at 350 degrees until heated through.

TUNA FLORENTINE

Donna Strong

2 (10-oz.) pkgs. frozen chopped
  spinach, thawed
2 T. instant minced onion
1 (12-oz.) can tuna, drained
6 eggs, hard-boiled, sliced
2 (10¾-oz.) cans condensed cream
  of mushroom soup

1 cup sour cream
salt and pepper
¼ cup butter, melted
2 cups soft bread crumbs (about
  4 slices)

Squeeze spinach to remove excess liquid. Spread spinach evenly in a greased 2 quart casserole. Sprinkle with onions, tuna and eggs. Mix mushroom soup and sour cream. Pour mixture evenly over eggs. Mix melted butter and crumbs and sprinkle evenly over top of casserole. 350 degrees for 30-35 minutes or until golden brown and bubbly. Recipe can be cut in half.

TURKEY-EGGPLANT CASSEROLE

Jennie Geisler
From the Erie Times–News

1¼ lb. ground skinless turkey
1 medium onion, chopped
3 cloves garlic, minced
1 large eggplant, cubed
1 (26-28 oz.) can crushed tomatoes
1 medium green bell pepper

1 medium red bell pepper
¾ cup seasoned dried bread
  crumbs
1 tsp. dried basil
¼ cup grated Parmesan cheese

Preheat oven to 350 degrees. Spray 13x9 baking pan with nonstick cooking spray. Spray a large, nonstick saucepan or Dutch oven with nonstick cooking spray, heat. Add turkey, onion and garlic. Cook, stirring as needed, until the turkey is browned and the onion is softened, 5 to 6 minutes. Add the eggplant, tomatoes, peppers, bread crumbs and basil. Bring to a boil, stirring as needed. Transfer the turkey mixture to the baking pan and bake, covered, until the vegetables are tender, about 45 minutes. Uncover and sprinkle with cheese. Bake until the cheese is lightly browned, about 15 minutes longer. Let stand 5 minutes before serving.

Recipe Note: Challenge anyone you know who hates eggplant to try this. They'll probably change their minds. Per serving, 189 calories, 2 grams fat, 3 grams fiber, 22 grams protein, 21 grams carbohydrate, 397 milligrams sodium, 46 milligrams cholesterol, 127 milligrams calcium. From Weight Watchers "Simply the Best."

WACKY CROCK POT ROAST

Caroline Mulson

1 beef roast, any cut, sized to fit into your crock pot (approx. 3 pounds)
1 pkg. dry Ranch salad dressing mix
1 pkg. dry brown gravy mix
1 pkg. dry Italian salad dressing mix
1 cup warm water

Place roast in crock pot. In a separate bowl, mix all three packages of dry mix together. Sprinkle on top of roast. Pour water in the bottom of the crock pot. Cook on low-heat setting for 6-8 hours.

Note: the gravy is flavorful accompaniment to mashed potatoes. Leftover meat is perfect for use in hot roast beef sandwiches. This is also an excellent way to prepare a venison roast.

Recipe Note: Makes a meal fit for a "King".

WHITE FISH PROVENCAL

Jennie Geisler
From the Erie Times–News

2 lb. (6 fillets) firm white fish, such as tilapia
1 T. olive oil
1 medium white onion, chopped
4 cloves garlic, minced
2 cups chopped tomatoes
1 (14½ - oz.) can large, pitted black olives, drained and sliced in half lengthwise
2 T. white wine, such as pinot gris
7 large leaves basil, torn
1 tsp. dried or 2 teaspoons fresh thyme

Preheat oven to 375 degrees. Coat ovenproof baking dish with nonstick cooking spay. Place fish in single layer in baking dish. Lightly salt and pepper. Bake 12 minutes. Meanwhile, heat oil in sauce pan. Add onion and garlic and sauté 5 minutes. Add tomatoes, olives, wine, basil and thyme. Simmer, uncovered over medium heat, 3 minutes. Remove fish from oven. Spoon sauce over fish. Return to oven and bake 5 more minutes or until fish flakes easily. Serves 6

Recipe Note: I'm including this one for my mom, because it's the recipe she makes the most out of any I've written. Even my dad likes it. They're both lifetime Weight Watchers, so it fits their diet and lifestyle well. Per fillet: 201 calories, 9 grams fat, 1 gram fiber, 25 grams protein, 5 grams carbohydrate, 477 milligrams sodium

ZUCCHINI CASSEROLE

Kathleen Dahl

Erie
Times-News

6 cups zucchini, diced
2 onions, diced
1 cup grated carrots
1 cup sour cream
1 cup cream of chicken soup

salt
pepper
1 box Stove Top stuffing mix
1 cup butter

Cook zucchini for 5 minutes and drain well. Combine onions, carrots, sour cream, soup, salt and pepper with zucchini. Prepare stuffing by adding one cup of butter. Place half of the stuffing mix into the bottom of a 9x13 casserole dish. Place zucchini mixture on top of that and top with remaining stuffing. Cover and bake at 350 degrees for 40-45 minutes.

ZUCCHINI MACASSA

Jade Conners
Carm Berquist – Mom

4 lbs. ground beef
20 med. zucchini, sliced (approx 6 lbs.)
6 med. tomato, diced
2 cloves garlic, minced
2 large onions, chopped (Mom uses less)

1 cup chili sauce
4 tsp. salt
1/2 tsp. pepper
1/2 tsp. allspice
1/2 tsp. cinnamon
1 lb. Monterey Jack, shredded
1/4 cup oil

In 5-quart Dutch oven over medium heat, cook beef, onion and garlic until meat is brown and onion is tender. Add tomato, chili sauce, salt, pepper, all spice and cinnamon and heat to boiling. Reduce heat to low and simmer uncovered for 45 minutes. Remove from heat and stir in 1/2 of cheese. Meanwhile, in 8-quart pan over medium-high heat, cook zucchini in hot oil, 1/2 at a time, for about 6 minutes, or until tender. Stir frequently, adding more oil if necessary. Preheat oven to 350 degrees. Makes 2 (9x13) pans. Layer 1/8 of zucchini on bottom of pan, top with 1/4 of meat. Repeat layer. End with zucchini. Sprinkle top with remaining cheese. Bake uncovered 25 minutes or until hot and bubbly.

Recipe Note: Can freeze for up to 3 months. Defrost in refrigerator overnight. Mom freezes after layering and does the baking after it is defrosted.

74987-06

ZUCCHINI PIZZA

Mary Butters

4 cups coarsely grated zucchini
1 tsp. salt
2 eggs, beaten
⅓ cup flour
½ cup grated mozzarella or
  cheddar cheese
½ cup grated Parmesan or
  Romano cheese

2 T. fresh basil
salt
pepper
½ cup tomato sauce
1 cup favorite grated cheese
favorite assorted pizza toppings

Put zucchini into colander, sprinkle with salt, toss and let sit for 30 minutes. Squeeze out excess moisture. Preheat oven to 350 degrees. In large mixing bowl combine zucchini, eggs, flour, cheeses, basil and season to taste with salt and pepper. Spread mixture into a lightly oiled 10" round or 13x9 rectangle pan. Bake 20-25 minutes or until surface is dry and beginning to brown. Broil for 5 minutes until top is firm and lightly browned. Remove from oven and spread tomato sauce on. Arrange with favorite toppings and sprinkle with cheese. Bake 10-15 minutes longer until cheese is melted and bubbling. Serves 8.

ZUCCHINI STUFFING CASSEROLE

Holly Graves

2 lbs. zucchini, peeled and cubed
¼ cup onion, diced
1 (10¾-oz.) can cream of chicken
  soup

1 (8-oz.) ctn. sour cream
1 cup shredded carrot
2 cups stuffing mix
¼ cup margarine, melted

Cook zucchini and onion in boiling, salted water for 5-10 minutes until crisp and tender. Drain well. Combine soup and sour cream. Stir in carrot. Fold in zucchini and onion. Mix well. Toss stuffing mix with margarine. Spread half the stuffing in a 11x7 pan. Spoon zucchini on top. Sprinkle with remaining stuffing. Bake 350 degrees for 25-30 minutes.

Erie
Times-News

74987-06

BREADS & ROLLS

AUTUMN SPICE BREAD

Jeremiah Mulson

3½ cups flour
2 tsp. baking soda
2 tsp. cinnamon
1 tsp. nutmeg
1 tsp. salt
½ tsp. ginger
½ tsp. cloves

1 cup butter
2 cups sugar
2 cups canned pumpkin
4 eggs, lightly whipped
1½ cups chocolate chips
1½ cups walnuts, chopped

Grease 2 loaf pans; set aside. Combine flour, soda and spices. Cream butter with sugar and pumpkin, blend in eggs. At low speed add dry ingredients to egg mixture. Mix in chocolate chips and one cup walnuts, stir to blend. Pour into loaf pans and sprinkle with ½ cup nuts. Bake at 350 degrees for 1 to 1½ hours, top with spice glaze. Makes 2 loaves.

SPICE GLAZE

1 cup powdered sugar
¼ tsp. nutmeg
¼ tsp. cinnamon

2-3 tsp. cream or milk
½ cup walnuts, chopped

Combine dry ingredients, blending in cream or milk until mixture becomes the consistency of glaze. Spread on loaves when removed from oven. Sprinkle with remaining nuts. After 5 minutes, remove from pans and cool on a rack.

BANANA BREAD

Marty Merritt
Mother–In–Law Marilyn Merritt

1 cup sugar
2 eggs
½ cup shortening
½ cup water
1 tsp. baking powder
1 tsp. baking soda

2 cups flour
3 bananas, mashed (not over-
   ripened)
½ cup chopped walnuts (if
   desired)

Grease and flour 1 large or 2 smaller bread pans. Mix together with an electric mixer, sugar, shortening, and eggs. Add mashed bananas. Then water. Mix in dry ingredients and nuts if desired. Pour into pan(s). Bake at 350 degrees for 1 hour. Remove from pans immediately and cool.

Recipe Note: I received this recipe from my mother-in-law when I was married in 1977. It is the best I've tried!

BLUEBERRY COFFEE CAKE

Susie Scott

Erie
Times-News

1 cup butter
2 cups sugar
2 eggs
1 cup sour cream
½ tsp. vanilla extract
1½ cups + 2 T. Flour
1 tsp. baking powder

¼ tsp. salt
1 cup fresh blueberries
½ cup brown sugar
1 tsp. cinnamon
1 cup chopped pecans
powdered sugar

Preheat the oven to 350 degrees. Grease and flour a Bundt pan. Cream the butter and sugar in a large bowl until soft, fluffy and well blended. Beat in the eggs, one at a time, the sour cream and the vanilla. Combine the flour, baking powder, and salt in a medium bowl and mix well. Add to the sour cream mixture; mix well. Fold in the blueberries. Combine the brown sugar, cinnamon and pecans in a small bowl and mix well. Spoon half of the batter into the Bundt pan and smooth it lightly with the back of a spoon. Top with the pecan mixture. Spoon in the remaining batter, smoothing it again. Bake for 50-60 minutes or until a toothpick inserted into it comes out clean. Cool in the pan on a wire rack for 10 minutes, then remove from pan. When cake is completely cooled, sprinkle with powdered sugar.

BLUEBERRY ORANGE BREAD

Dawn Blackburn

2 cups flour
1 cup sugar
1 tsp. baking powder
½ tsp. baking soda
½ tsp. salt
1 egg

½ cup orange juice
⅓ cup water
2 T. melted butter or margarine
2 tsp. grated orange peel
¾ cup fresh or frozen blueberries

Combine first five ingredients in a large bowl. In a smaller bowl mix together the next four ingredients and combine with the dry ingredients until just moistened. Fold in blueberries. Pour into a greased and floured loaf pan and bake at 350 degrees for 65 to 70 minutes, or until a toothpick inserted in the middle comes out clean. Cool 10 minutes before removing from pan. Slices easier when completely cool.

74987-06

BRIOCHE

Marnie Mead Oberle
Adapted from
The Bread Machine Cookbook

1 cup milk
¼ cup butter (do not substitute
  margarine), nonsalted
2 eggs
3 T. sugar

1 T. salt
3 cups flour, unbleached
2 tsp. yeast
½ cup chocolate chips or nuts or
  candied fruit (optional)

Combine all ingredients except the add-ins (chocolate chips, etc.) in your bread machine and put on dough setting. When done, combine mix-ins if you desire (adding more or less depending on your taste). You can then make one traditional brioche, or divide into 12 large balls and 12 mini balls. Place dough into brioche pan, or muffin tins, press down top with your thumb in center, and put small ball on top. Let rise, covered, for about an hour. Brush with beaten egg and sprinkle with some sugar. Bake at 400 degrees for 25-30 minutes for large brioche, about 12-15 minutes for the smaller ones.

Recipe Note: This recipe is great when you are having houseguests or for a brunch. Because of the beauty of the brioche pan, you can take the top off and hollow out the inside to put in a dip. The pieces from the inside can be used for dipping. Day-old brioche also makes great French toast!

BURST O' LEMON BREAD

Pat Bablak

1¾ cups all-purpose flour
¾ cup sugar
1 tsp. baking powder
¾ tsp. baking soda
¼ tsp. salt
1 (8-oz.) carton lemon yogurt

1 egg
⅓ cup margarine
1 T. grated lemon peel
1 T. lemon juice
½ cup coconut

In a large bowl, sift together the flour, sugar, baking powder, baking soda and salt. In another bowl, beat the yogurt, egg, margarine, lemon peel and lemon juice until smooth; stir into dry ingredients just until moistened. Fold in coconut. Fill well-greased and floured loaf pan. Bake at 350 degrees until top of bread shows no moisture. Cool for 5 minutes before removing from pan. Poke holes using a toothpick all around top of cake for glaze.

GLAZE

¾ cup sugar
¼ cup lemon juice from real
  lemon

½ tsp. vanilla

Heat in small pan until mixture comes to a boil, then cook for a minute or so. Pour mixture over bread and remove from pan when cake is cooled.

CINNAMON BREAD

Sandra Yonko

½ cup margarine
1 cup sugar
2 eggs
1 tsp. vanilla
1 cup sour cream

¼ cup milk
2 cup flour
1½ tsp. baking powder
1 tsp. baking soda

CINNAMON MIXTURE

1 T. cinnamon

½ cup sugar

Blend all ingredients except cinnamon mixture and put half in loaf pans. Make sure to grease and flour pans. Sprinkle ½ the cinnamon mixture on top and then spoon remaining dough over. Cover with remaining cinnamon mixture. Cut through batter with a knife. Bake at 350 degrees about 30 to 50 minutes, depending on the size of the pan. Will make 2 small regular loaves or 4 mini loaves.

CRANBERRY-BANANA BREAD

Mary Agnes Mosher

2 cups fresh or frozen cranberries
1 cup sugar
1 cup water
⅓ cup margarine
⅔ cup sugar
2 eggs

1¾ cups flour
2 tsp. baking powder
½ tsp. salt
¼ tsp. baking soda
1⅓ cups ripe bananas, mashed
½ cup chopped walnuts

Preheat oven to 350 degrees. Combine cranberries, 1 cup sugar, and water; cook 5 minutes over medium heat or until cranberries begin to split. Drain and set aside. Cream margarine and ⅔ cup sugar, beat until mixture is fluffy. Add eggs, one at a time, beating well after each. Sift together all dry ingredients. Add dry ingredients to creamed mixture alternately with bananas. Blend thoroughly. Fold in by hand the cooked cranberries and nuts. Spoon batter into greased and floured pan(s): ether one 9x5 or two small loaf pans. Bake 45-55 minutes for large pan - 35 minutes for small loaf pans OR until center tests done with a toothpick. Cool in pans for 5 minutes; remove to wire rack and cool completely.

74987-06

DELICIOUS PUMPKIN BREAD

Lois Fobes

3¼ cups all-purpose flour
2 tsp. baking soda
2 tsp. ground cinnamon
2 cups solid pack pumpkin purée
1 cup vegetable oil

1 tsp. salt
3 cups white sugar
⅔ cup water
4 eggs

Grease and flour three 7x3 inch pans. Preheat oven to 350 degrees. Measure flour, sugar, baking soda, salt and cinnamon into large bowl. Stir to blend. Add pumpkin, water, salad oil, eggs. Beat until well combined. Pour batter into prepared pans. (Optional - you can add ½ cup chopped walnuts or ½ cup chocolate chips to batter.) Bake for approximately 1 hour.

ENGLISH SCONE

Melissa Lesniewski

2 cups all-purpose flour
2 tsp. baking powder
2 T. granulated sugar
½ tsp. salt

⅓ cup butter, chilled and cut into
½-inch pieces
½ cup milk
1 large egg, beaten

GLAZE

1 large egg, beaten

1 T. milk

Preheat oven to 400 degrees. For the glaze, mix together beaten egg with the milk; set aside. In a large bowl, whisk together flour, baking powder, sugar and salt. In a measuring cup, combine the milk with the beaten egg. With a pastry blender, or your fingertips, rub the butter into the flour mixture until it resembles coarse crumbs. Make a well in the center of the dry ingredients and add the liquid. Mix together with a wooden spoon, making sure you do not over-work the dough. Just mix until the dough forms moist clumps. Gather dough together and transfer to a lightly floured surface. Gently knead dough until it forms a ball (10 seconds). Pat down dough until it is ¾-inch thick. With a floured 2-inch cutter cut out rounds and place on baking pan. Knead together scraps and cut out remaining scones. Brush scones with glaze and bake for 15 minutes or until lightly brown on top. Remove from oven and cool on wire rack. Makes 12 scones.

HOBO BREAD

Sister Irene Warchol
Contributed by Rhonda Schember

3 cups seedless raisins
4 tsp. baking soda
2½ cups boiling water
2 cups sugar
2 eggs
3 T. oil

½ tsp. salt
4 cup flour
2 tsp. baking powder
1 tsp. vanilla
1 cup chopped nuts

Mix together raisins, baking soda and boiling water. Let stand overnight. Blend remaining ingredients into raisin mixture. Pour into greased and floured loaf pans. Bake in 350 degrees oven for 30 minutes, then 325 degrees oven for 15 minutes. Makes 3 loaves.

IRISH BREAD

Marty Merritt
Grandma Martha Black

3 cups flour
¼ cup sugar
1 tsp. baking soda
1 tsp. baking powder
1 tsp. salt

¼ tsp. cream of tartar
1 cup raisins
1½ cups buttermilk
1 T. melted butter

Sift dry ingredients. Add raisins, buttermilk and melted butter. Mix together to form a sticky dough. Place dough on floured surface and knead gently. Place in a greased 9-inch pan. Bake at 450 degrees for 25 minutes. Best served the first day.

Recipe Note: This is an original family recipe from Ireland and my Irish Grandma, who came to the United States in 1914 through Ellis Island.

74987-06

MAMA BUNS

Ann Carson
Steph Reid's favorite!

3 cups warm water, between 105
  and 115 degrees
1½ pkgs. instant dry yeast
1½ tsp. salt

¾ cup sugar
½ cup Crisco solid shortening
2 eggs, slightly beaten
8 to 9 cups all-purpose flour

Combine yeast, water, salt, sugar, Crisco and beaten eggs. Stir. Add flour, 3 cups at a time. Let rise one hour in a warm, draft free area. Punch down. Repeat every hour for 3 more hours. On the fourth punch, shape into rolls. Place on a greased cookie sheet. Cover with tea towels and then a large plastic garbage bag over all. Let rise over night or 10 to 12 hours. Bake at 350 degrees for 15 to 20 minutes. I get 15 buns on a large cookie sheet, 30 in all.

Recipe Note: I always start these buns after supper and then Steph and her Dad have a delightful breakfast! What a way to wake up with the smell of fresh bread in the house. These are wonderful for sandwiches too.

POPPY SEED BREAD

Nancy Phillips

3 cups flour
2¾ cups sugar
1½ tsp. salt
1½ tsp. baking powder
1 tsp. almond extract
1 tsp. vanilla extract
1 tsp. tsp. butter extract (optional)
3 eggs

1½ cups milk
1½ cups oil
2 T. poppy seeds
¼ cup orange juice
¾ cup confectionary sugar
½ tsp. almond extract
½ tsp. vanilla

Mix dry ingredients, eggs, oil, milk, flavorings and poppy seed and blend 2 minutes. Bake in greased and floured bread tins (1 large, 2 medium or 4 small tins). Bake in 350 degree oven for 40 minutes to 1 hour depending on the loaf size. Glaze: Mix orange juice, confectionary sugar, almond extract and vanilla in small saucepan. Bring to boil; simmer 4 to 5 minutes. Do not over cook. Brush on loaves direct from oven. Freezes well.

POPPY SEED BREAD

Pat Bablak

Erie
Times-News

1⅛ cups vegetable oil
3 eggs
2½ cups sugar
1½ T. poppy seed
1½ cups milk

1½ tsp. each of vanilla and
  almond extracts
3 cups flour
1 tsp. salt
1½ tsp. baking powder

Whisk first 6 ingredients until well-blended, then sift together the flour, salt and baking powder into the mix until moistened. Pour into 2 medium-sized well-greased and floured loaf pan and bake at 350 degrees until moisture is gone from top of breads. Poke holes with a toothpick on breads for glaze.

GLAZE

¾ cup sugar
¼ cup orange juice

½ tsp. almond extract
½ tsp. vanilla extract

Heat above ingredients in a small pan. Cook a minute or so after mixture starts to boil and pour over bread. Remove from pans when cool.

PUMPKIN RIBBON BREAD

Caroline Mulson

FILLING

1 (6-oz.) pkg. cream cheese,
  softened
⅓ cup sugar

1 T. flour
1 egg
2 T. grated orange peel

Beat cream cheese, sugar and flour together in a small bowl; add egg and mix to blend. Stir in orange peel, set aside.

BREAD

1 cup cooked pumpkin
½ cup vegetable oil
2 eggs
1½ cups sugar
½ tsp. salt

½ tsp. cloves
½ tsp. cinnamon
1⅔ cups flour
1 tsp. baking soda
1 cup chopped nuts

Combine pumpkin, oil and eggs in a large bowl. Add sugar, salt, cloves, cinnamon, flour, soda and pecans; mix to blend. Pour ¼ of batter into 2 greased loaf pans. Carefully spread filling over batter and add remaining batter to cover filling. Bake at 325 degrees for 1½ hours. Cool 10 minutes. Remove from pans. Store in refrigerator.

74987-06

RASPBERRY BANANA MUFFINS

Dana Kluz

2 cups flour
½ tsp. baking powder
¾ tsp. baking soda
¼ tsp. salt
¼ lb. butter
1 cup sugar

2 eggs
3 over-ripe bananas
¼ cup sour cream
1 tsp. vanilla
1 pt. fresh raspberries

Preheat oven to 350 degrees. Mix together dry ingredients. Cream butter with sugar until fluffy. Beat in eggs. Purée bananas, sour cream and vanilla. Alternate and add dry ingredients and banana mixture to the egg mixture. Beat to incorporate. Fold in raspberries. Spoon into greased muffin tins and bake for about 25 minutes until puffy, golden and springy. Makes about 15 large muffins.

SOUR CREAM BANANA BREAD WITH CHOCOLATE GLAZE

Ramona Piazza

½ cup butter, room temperature
1¼ cups sugar
2 eggs
½ cup sour cream
1 tsp. vanilla
1 cup mashed ripe bananas (about
  2 medium)

1¾ cups flour
1 tsp. baking soda
1 tsp. baking powder
pinch salt
½ cup semi-sweet chocolate chips
  (can use mini chips)
¾ cup chopped nuts

Beat together first six ingredients until blended. Stir in remaining ingredients until dry ingredients are just moistened. Do not over-mix. Divide batter between 4 greased and lightly floured mini loaf pans and bake at 325 degrees for 45-50 minutes or until a cake tester inserted in center comes out clean. Allow to cool in pans for about 15 minutes and then remove from pans and continue cooling on a rack. When cool, drizzle tops with Chocolate Glaze. Yields 4 mini loaves.

GLAZE

½ cup semi-sweet chocolate chips,   3 T. butter, melted
  melted

Stir together chocolate and butter until well blended.

STRAWBERRY YOGURT SCONES

Jennie Geisler
From the Erie Times–News

1½ cups all-purpose flour
⅔ cup whole-wheat flour
½ cup sugar
2 tsp. baking powder
½ tsp. salt
¾ cup diced strawberries
⅔ cup plain, fat-free yogurt

3 T. butter, melted
½ tsp. grated rind of orange,
    tangerine or clementine
1 large egg white, lightly beaten
cooking spray
2 tsp. sugar

Preheat oven to 400 degrees. Lightly spoon flours into dry measuring cups and level with a knife. Combine flours, ½ cup sugar, baking powder and salt in a large bowl. Combine strawberries, yogurt, butter, rind and egg white; add to flour mixture, stirring just until moist. Turn dough out onto a lightly floured surface; knead lightly 4 times with floured hands. Pat into an 8-inch circle on a baking sheet coated with cooking spray. Score dough into 12 wedges, and sprinkle with 2 teaspoons sugar. Bake at 400 degrees for 20 to 25 minutes, or until lightly browned. Makes 12 scones

Recipe Note: You might remember I had a small problem with this recipe, adapted from Cooking Light magazine in December 2002, in that I could not stop making these. Update: I still can't stop making these. Per scone: 152 calories, 3.3 grams fat, 3.6 grams protein, 27.7 grams carbohydrate, 1.5 grams fiber, 1.1 milligrams iron, 227 milligrams sodium, 78 milligrams calcium

Recipe Favorites

74987-06

DESSERTS

"KRAZY" CAKE

Olivia Balczon

1½ cups flour	1 T. vinegar
1 cup sugar	1 tsp. vanilla
⅓ cup cocoa	⅓ cup Mazola oil
½ tsp. salt	1 cup cold water
1 tsp. baking soda	

Put dry ingredients in an 8-" or 9-inch pan. With a tablespoon, make 3 holes. In one hole, put vinegar; in the other, put vanilla; in the 3rd hole, put oil. Pour 1 cup of water over whole mixture and mix until all is wet. Bake at 350 degrees for about 20-30 minutes or judge. Double for 13x9 pan.

12 LAYER RAINBOW JELL-O

Debra Hull

2 (3-oz.) boxes lemon Jell-O	1 (3-oz.) box cherry Jell-O
1 (3-oz.) box orange Jell-O	1 (3-oz.) box raspberry Jell-O
1 (3-oz.) box lime Jell-O	1 (16-oz.) ctn. sour cream

Dissolve 1 package of Jell-O in 1 cup of boiling water. Divide in half and add 4 tablespoons cold water in one part and pour into a lightly buttered pan and refrigerate until firm. Stir in ⅓ cup of sour cream into the other half of the Jell-O until smooth. Pour over first layer after it has cooled. Do this for each Jell-O flavor, layering as you go. Start and finish with lemon Jell-O.

Recipe Note: This dessert has more decorative appeal when prepared in a clear glass bowl or dish.

5 LAYERED BANANA PINEAPPLE DESSERT
(May 2005 Cook of the Week Recipe)

Marty Merritt

Erie
Times-News

1½ cups graham cracker crumbs
¼ cup sugar
⅓ cup margarine or butter (melted)
3 to 4 bananas (sliced)
1 (8-oz.) pkg. cream cheese (lite or fat free)

3½ cups milk
2 4 Serving pkgs. vanilla instant pudding (fat free or sugar free)
1 (20-oz.) can crushed pineapple (well drained)
1 (8-oz.) ctn. Cool Whip (lite or fat free)

Crust - Melt margarine in 13x9 pan. Add crumbs and sugar. Press evenly in bottom of pan. Slice bananas on top of crust. Beat softened cream cheese with wire whisk until smooth. Gradually beat in milk. Mixture may be lumpy. Add dry pudding mixes and mix until thickened. Spread over bananas. Spread well-drained pineapple over pudding. Spread Cool Whip over top. Chill 3 hours. Cut into 12-15 squares.

A GOOD-FOR-YOU CUPCAKE

Jacque Mulson

1 cup crushed pineapple in its own juice
3 cups flour
2 cups sugar
1 tsp. baking soda
1 tsp. baking powder
1 tsp. salt

2 tsp. cinnamon
2 lg. eggs
1 egg white
½ cup safflower oil
2 tsp. vanilla extract
2 cups coarsely shredded carrots
½ cup applesauce

Heat the oven to 350 degrees. Drain the pineapple and reserve the juice. In a large bowl, whisk together the flour, sugar, baking soda, baking powder, salt and cinnamon. Make a well in the center of the mixture and drop in the eggs, egg white, oil, vanilla extract, and reserved pineapple juice. Beat at medium speed until blended, about 1½ minutes. With a spoon, stir in the crushed pineapple, shredded carrots, and applesauce. Then spoon the batter into paper bake cups set in 2 muffin tins. Bake until a toothpick stuck in the center of a cupcake comes out clean, about 22 minutes. Remove the tins from the oven and cool on a wire rack for 2 minutes. Serve warm. Makes 24 cupcakes.

74987-06

ALMOND PUFF

Nancy Phillips

½ cup oleo or butter   2 T. water
I cup flour

Heat oven to 350 degrees. Cut ½ cup butter/oleo into I cup flour. Sprinkle 2 T. water over mixture; mix with fork. Round into ball; divide in half. On ungreased cookie sheet pat each half into a strip 12x3-inch strip. Strips should be about 3 inches apart.

FILLING

½ cup oleo or butter   I cup flour
I cup water   3 eggs
I tsp. almond extract

In medium saucepan heat ½ cup butter/oleo and I cup water to rolling boil. Remove from heat and quickly stir in almond extract and I cup flour. Stir vigorously over low heat. Beat in eggs all at once until smooth. Divide in half; spreading each half evenly over strips, covering completely. Bake 50 to 55 minutes our until topping is crisp and brown. Cool.

FROSTING

1½ cups powdered sugar   I to 1½ tsp. almond extract
2 tsp. oleo or butter   1-2 T. water

Combine. Frost when cool. Top with sliced almonds, if desired. Cut into I-inch strips.

Recipe Note: An easy recipe that is always a hit.

APPLE (ZUCCHINI) CRISP

Mandy Barney

FILLING

8 cups sliced, peeled zucchini   I cup sugar
   (remove seeds)   ½ tsp. nutmeg
⅔ cup lemon juice   I tsp. cinnamon

Cook zucchini in lemon juice until tender, 10-15 minutes, then add sugar, nutmeg & cinnamon. Simmer I more minute. Add ½ cup crust mixture to thicken.

CRUST

4 cups flour   3 sticks butter/oleo
1½ cups sugar

Press ½ mixture in 11x16 cookie sheet. Bake 10 minutes at 375 degrees. Put filling over baked crust. Add I teaspoon cinnamon to remaining mixture. Sprinkle this over filling then pat lightly. Then bake 375 degrees for 30-40 minutes.

APPLE BUTTER PUMPKIN PIE

Sandy Reid
Grandma Clara

Erie
Times-News

1 cup apple butter
1 cup fresh or canned pumpkin
½ cup packed brown sugar
½ tsp. salt
¾ tsp. ground cinnamon
¾ tsp. ground nutmeg

⅛ tsp. ground ginger
3 large eggs, slightly beaten
¾ cup evaporated milk
1 unbaked 9-inch pie shell
whipped cream for garnish

Preheat oven to 425 degrees. Combine apple butter, pumpkin, sugar, salt and spices in a bowl Stir in eggs. Gradually add milk and mix well. Pour into the pie shell. Bake for about 40 minutes or until set.

Recipe Note: If the crust begins to get too brown, place a strip of tin foil around the crimped edge of the crust and lower the temperature in the oven.

APPLE DESSERT

Carolyn Jack

1 cup flour
⅓ tsp. salt
½ tsp. soda
½ cup brown sugar

1 cup quick oats
½ cup shortening
2½ cups sliced apples
½ cup white sugar

Stir together apples and white sugar. Set aside. Mix together flour, salt, soda, brown sugar, and quick oats. Into this mixture cut in the ½ cup of shortening. Place half of the dry mixture into a buttered baking pan. Press down firmly. Place sugared apples on top and dot with butter. Cover with remainder of dry mixture. Bake for 40-45 minutes at 350 degrees. Serve warm or cold with whipped topping or ice cream. Can also be sprinkled with cinnamon if desired.

BANANA SPLIT CAKE

Linda Heck

2 cups graham crackers
1 stick melted butter
2 cups powdered sugar
2 eggs
1 tsp. vanilla
4 oz. cream cheese

½ stick butter
3 bananas
1 (20-oz.) can crushed pineapple,
  drained
1 large tub Cool Whip

Mix together the graham crackers and stick of melted butter, then press into a 9x13 pan. Beat the ½ stick of butter, cream cheese, eggs, vanilla and powdered sugar until smooth and creamy. Spread on the graham cracker layer. Slice bananas, and add to the second layer. Put the drained pineapple on top of the bananas. Spread the Cool Whip over the pineapple, and top with crushed nuts and cut up cherries. Cool for 1 hour before serving.

74987-06

BANANA SPLIT DESSERT

Holly Graves

CRUST

2 cups graham cracker crumbs	1 stick margarine, melted

Mix together and press into bottom of a 9x13 pan.

FILLING

2 sticks margarine, at room temperature	pinch salt
2 cups powdered sugar	5 bananas, sliced lengthwise
2 eggs	1 cup pineapple, drained (saving juice)
1 tsp. vanilla	

Beat together all filling ingredients, except for bananas and pineapple, for 5 minutes. Pour over crust. Dip bananas in juice. Place on creamed filling mixture. Sprinkle crushed pineapple over bananas. Top with Cool Whip, maraschino cherries and nuts.

BERRY PIE

Pat Veltri

2 cups berries (any kind)	2 T. tapioca
1 cup sugar (I used Splenda this year)	2 T. lemon juice
	2 T. melted butter

Mix ingredients together. Let stand 15 minutes. If baked immediately: 425 degrees for 15 minutes then lower temperature to 350 degrees for 40 minutes or until crust is browned (I have never baked the pie immediately, so I really can't attest to the baking temperatures). Don't forget to put foil around the edges before putting in the oven. I do this even with the frozen pie. For frozen pies: Do not puncture top before freezing. I use the Hefty 2.5 gallon bags. When ready to bake: Do not preheat oven. Put frozen pie in at start. I make slits in the pie and wrap foil around the edges, put the pie in the oven, turn it on to 350 degrees and bake for about 1 hour.

Recipe Note: I use this recipe for blueberry pies as well as raspberry pies and have never been disappointed. Hope you will try it once. It's so easy and I never adjust the ingredients. Happy Baking!

BETTER-THAN-SEX CAKE

Mary Simpson

1 box Dutch chocolate cake mix
(or dark chocolate, devil's food)
1 (14-oz.) can Eagle brand
sweetened condensed milk
1 1-pint jar Mrs. Richardson's
caramel fudge topping (or just
caramel)

1 large container Cool Whip
3 ground up Heath bars

Make cake as directed on box and bake, as directed. When done (while cake is still warm) poke holes in cake with end of wooden spoon. Pour sweetened condensed milk over cake. Pour caramel fudge topping over cake. When caked has cooled, frost with Cool Whip and sprinkle with Heath bars. Refrigerate.

Recipe Note: Can be served immediately. Gets soggy after it's more than a day old, but it still tastes good!

BLUEBERRY CHEESECAKE YUM

Jennie Geisler
From the Erie Times–News

1 reduced-fat graham cracker pie
crust
2 T. butter, melted
1 (8-oz.) pkg. reduced-fat cream
cheese, softened
1 cup Splenda

¼ tsp. salt
2 tsp. vanilla extract
½ tsp. lemon juice
1 (8-oz.) tub frozen whipped
topping, thawed
3 cups blueberries

Into a medium bowl, slide the crust out of the pan and crush together with the butter. Sprinkle evenly into the bottom of a 8- or 9-inch square baking dish, and pack down with a pancake turner into a solid crust. In a large bowl, beat cream cheese with Splenda until smooth. Stir in salt and lemon juice. Fold in the whipped topping until well-blended, then fold in the blueberries. Spoon over the crust in the baking dish and spread evenly. Cover with plastic wrap and refrigerate for at least 1 hour before serving. Makes 9 1-cup servings

Recipe Note: This is the recipe that's most requested from my stash. My girlfriends clamor for it at every gathering, and its sweet taste and soft texture holds up to any amount of abuse by sloppy partygoers and forgetful hosts. Don't ask how I know that. Per cup: 220 calories, 12.3 grams fat, 1.2 grams fiber, 12.8 grams protein, 26.8 grams carbohydrate, 242 milligrams sodium

74987-06

BLUEBERRY RHUBARB PIE

Victoria Brogdon

FILLING

2 cups blueberries	1⅓ cups sugar
2 cups cut rhubarb	⅓ cup instant tapioca

Heat the oven to 425 degrees. Wash blueberries, removing any remaining stems. Wash rhubarb and cut into 1-inch pieces. Drain both well. Mix all ingredients together and let sit while preparing the pie dough. Stir occasionally to help bring out the juices. Prepare pie dough for a 9-inch pie plate. Add the blueberry rhubarb filling to the crust-lined pie plate. Wet the edge of the bottom piece of crust before placing the top piece in order to help seal edges. Before placing the top crust, cut slits in it using a decorative pattern. Using a fork or your fingers, seal the edges together. Cover the edge with 1½-inch strip of aluminum foil to prevent overly browning the edge. Bake about 50 minutes or until juice begins to bubble through the slits in the top crust. Remove the aluminum foil about five minutes before removing pie from oven so that the pie crust is evenly golden brown. Cool for a few hours before serving.

CRUST

2 cups flour	8 T. Crisco, trans fat free
½ tsp. salt	¼ cup orange juice
4 T. unsalted butter	

Mix flour and salt in a bowl. Cut butter into teaspoon-size slices and add to flour. Add the shortening. Using your hands, press the mixture between your thumb and fingers making flakes until the mixture is mealy. Add ¼ cup orange juice and mix with a fork until the dough clumps together; extra can be added about a tablespoon at a time until it just holds together. Divide the dough in about half, one piece being slightly larger than the other. You will use the large piece for the bottom of the pie plate and the smaller piece for the top. Gather dough together with hands and form a flat dough patty. For ease of handling, if you have time, wrap dough patties in waxed paper and refrigerate until chilled. Roll out dough on a flour-covered surface, such as a pastry cloth, with a rolling pin covered with a pastry cloth tube also rubbed with flour.

Recipe Note: Fresh, Erie area blueberries and rhubarb make the best pie! Both are available at the Griswold farmers' market. Rhubarb is best in the spring, so buy some and freeze it while waiting for the freshest blueberries in August.

BUDAPEST TEA BREAD

Maureen Bemko

Erie
Times-News

½ cup brown sugar
3 T. cocoa
3 T. cinnamon
1½ sticks margarine
1½ cups sugar
1 tsp. vanilla extract
2 eggs, slightly beaten

2½ cups flour
1 tsp. baking soda
1 tsp. baking powder
1 pinch salt
1 (14-oz.) carton sour cream,
   regular or low fat
6 shakes powdered sugar, sifted

Preheat oven to 350 degrees. Grease and flour a large Bundt pan and set aside. In a small bowl, combine brown sugar, cocoa, and cinnamon; set aside. In large bowl, cream together margarine and sugar. Add vanilla and eggs, mixing to blend. In a separate bowl, sift together flour, baking soda, baking powder, and salt. Add dry ingredients to the creamed mixture in the large bowl; mix well. Add sour cream and mix to blend. By hand, stir in the brown sugar mixed with cocoa and cinnamon. Spoon or pour the batter into prepared Bundt pan and bake 50 to 60 minutes. Cool in pan 10 to 15 minutes. Invert on cake plate that has two sheets of waxed paper placed on it to meet in the middle. Shake powdered sugar over cake and carefully removed waxed paper sheets with excess sugar.

Recipe Note: This deliciously different cake is a superb hybrid of gingerbread and chocolate cake. It is dense with flavor and pairs beautifully with a pot of strong Earl Grey tea.

BUTTER & NUT POUND CAKE

Mary Simpson

3 cups sugar
½ cup Crisco
2 sticks margarine
¼ tsp. salt
5 large eggs

1 small can evaporated milk (add
   water to make it equal 1 cup)
3 cups flour
2 T. vanilla butter and nut
   flavoring (no substitutions)

Cream shortening, sugar and salt. Add eggs, one at a time. Add flour and milk; alternating. End with flour. Fold in flavoring. Bake in greased, floured bundt pan. Start in cold oven turned to 325 degrees. Do not open door. Bake 1 hour 45 minutes. Cool 15 minutes and remove from pan.

74987-06

BUTTERSCOTCH SUPREME

Holly Graves

1 box yellow cake mix	2 eggs
1 can Thank You butterscotch pudding	

Mix all of the above by hand for 3 minutes. Spread in a slightly greased 9x13 pan.

TOPPING

1/3 cup granulated white sugar	1/2 cup chopped walnuts
6 oz. butterscotch chips	

Mix topping ingredients together and sprinkle over cake batter. Bake at 350 degrees for 35 minutes or until cake tests done.

Recipe Note: For Chocolate Supreme, use chocolate cake mix, chocolate pudding and chocolate chips.

CARMEL DIP FOR APPLES

Sandy Reid
Annie Carson and Gertie Reid

2 (8-oz.) pkg. Philadelphia cream cheese	crushed dry roasted peanuts
1 (12-oz.) jar Smucker's caramel ice cream topping	

Soften cream cheese (2 to 3 minutes in microwave on 50 percent power does nicely). Mix with 3/4 jar of topping. Spread in serving dish and let sit overnight in the refrigerator. Just before serving, swirl in remainder of the topping. Sprinkle with crushed peanuts. Dip sliced apples in mix and enjoy.

Recipe Note: This treat has tickled the fancy of many teachers!

CHOCOLATE COCONUT MACADAMIA NUT PIE

Linda Heck

2 eggs	1 cup white and chocolate swirled chips
1 stick butter	3/4 cup coconut
1/2 cup flour	3/4 cup macadamia nuts
1/2 cup sugar	
1/2 cup brown sugar	

Beat eggs, butter, flour, and both sugars on high speed until fluffy. Stir in the chips, coconut, and macadamia nuts. Then place into a prepared pie shell. Bake for 50-55 minutes at 325 degrees. Cool before serving.

CHOCOLATE PICNIC CAKE

Peggy Craig

I cup chopped dates (these come pre-chopped, in 2 cup bags)	1½ cup water I tsp. baking soda

Mix above ingredients together in a sauce pan. Bring to a boil, then cool. Add to cake mixture below.

CAKE

I cup sugar	1¾ cups flour
¾ cup shortening	½ tsp. salt
2 eggs	
2 T. unsweetened cocoa powder (I use Hershey's)	

Mix above ingredients together in a bowl. Add dates (with water) to the above mixture and mix thoroughly. Pour mixture into a floured and greased 9x12" cake pan. Bake at 350 degrees for 30-35 minutes. (Check with a toothpick or cake tester). Cake is a great "do ahead" - freezes very well. On occasion, I've made this in two pieces - two 9x9 or 8x8 pans (baking time is about the same, but watch), then shared one piece and eaten or frozen the other. It is NOT especially good warm and right from the oven - tastes MUCH better completely cooled.

TOPPING

chocolate chips	sugar
chopped walnuts	

Sprinkle top of batter with chocolate bits, chopped walnuts, and white granulated sugar. (Cake needs some sort of topping. If you don't want to use nuts, try using shredded coconut or maybe coarsely crushed hard cookies - Use your imagination!)

Recipe Note: This recipe is one of my mother's (Eunice Gillies). I don't remember from where it came originally, but we've been enjoying it since I was a child. We hope you like it as much as my brothers (who still live in Erie) and I do!

74987-06

CHOCOLATE SQUARES
Karen Churchill

3 sticks margarine
1½ cups brown sugar
1 egg
3 cups flour

2 tsp. vanilla
chocolate frosting or 12 oz. bag of
   chocolate chips

Cream margarine, brown sugar and egg. Add flour and vanilla. Mix well and spread onto greased 15x10 jelly-roll pan with sides on it. Dough is very soft. You may need to flour your fingers to spread dough on pan that has been greased. Bake 350 degrees for 15 minutes, no longer. You may frost with your favorite chocolate frosting or, while still hot, pour on a 12-ounce bag of chocolate chips and spread the melted chips out with a knife. Cool and cut in squares. Makes 6-7 dozen.

COCONUT POUND CAKE
Mary Agnes Mosher

1 stick butter or margarine
½ cup shortening
4 eggs
2 cups flour
2 tsp. baking powder

1 tsp. vanilla
1½ cups sugar
½ cup milk
1⅓ cups flaked coconut

DO NOT PREHEAT OVEN! Lightly blend all ingredients with electric mixer, then beat all ingredients except coconut at medium speed for 15 minutes. Scrape bowl occasionally. Blend in coconut thoroughly. Pour batter into ungreased tube pan; place on oven rack in middle of oven. NOW turn oven to 350 degrees. Bake for 45 minutes or longer until cake tests done with toothpick. Cool in pan for 15 minutes. Run knife around outside of pan. Remove tube section from pan and cool completely.

COTTAGE CHEESE FLUFF
Sherry R. Letzelter

1 cup small-curd cottage cheese
1 (3-oz.) pkg. orange Jell-O
1 (11-oz.) can mandarin oranges,
   drained
1 cup unsweetened crushed
   pineapple, drained

½ cup chopped pecans (optional)
1 (8-oz.) carton Cool Whip,
   thawed

In a bowl, combine the cottage cheese and Jell-O powder; mix well. Stir in oranges, pineapple, and pecans. Just before serving, fold in Cool Whip.

Recipe Note: A family favorite. Quick & easy to make.

CRANBERRY-GINGER CRUMBLE CAKE

Ramona Piazza

Erie
Times-News

2 cups fresh or frozen cranberries
1½ cups sugar
1 T. cornstarch
1½ tsp. grated lemon rind
¾ cup water
¾ cup all-purpose flour
¼ cup sugar
¼ cup cold butter, cut into pieces
½ cup crystallized ginger, finely chopped
1 (8-oz.) pkg. cream cheese, softened

½ cup butter or margarine, softened
¾ cup sugar
2 eggs
2 cups all-purpose flour
1½ cups tsp. baking powder
½ tsp. baking soda
½ tsp. salt
¼ cup milk
½ tsp. vanilla extract

Stir together first 4 ingredients in a saucepan; stir in water. Bring to a boil; reduce heat and simmer, uncovered, for 25 minutes or until cranberry skins pop and mixture is thickened. Remove from heat; set aside to cool. Combine ¾ cup flour, ¼ cup sugar and ¼ cup butter with a pastry blender or 2 knives until crumbly. Stir in ginger; set aside. Beat cream cheese and ½ cup butter at medium speed with an electric mixer until creamy; gradually add ¾ cup sugar, beating well. Add eggs, one at a time, beating until blended after each addition. Combine 2 cups flour and next 3 ingredients; add to cream cheese mixture alternately with milk, beginning and ending with flour mixture. Beat at low speed until blended after each addition. Stir in vanilla. Spoon half of batter into a greased 13x9 pan. Spread reserved cranberry mixture over batter. Drop remaining batter by rounded tablespoonfuls over cranberry mixture. Sprinkle with ginger topping. Bake at 350 degrees for 32-35 minutes or until toothpick inserted in center comes out clean. Cool in pan on a wire rack. Makes 12 servings.

CREAMY VANILLA PUDDING

Donna Strong

½ cup sugar
3 T. cornstarch
1 pinch salt
2½ cups milk

2 egg yolks, beaten
1 T. butter
1 tsp. vanilla

In saucepan, combine sugar, cornstarch & salt. Stir in milk until smooth. Bring to a boil over medium heat. Reduce heat-cook and stir for 2 minutes. Add ½ cup milk mixture to yolks. Return all to pan. Cook and stir for 1 minute or until thickened. Stir in butter and vanilla. 4 servings. You can also beat the egg whites until stiff, and add to cooled pudding. This makes it creamy and fluffy.

74987-06

CUPCAKE "ICE CREAM" CONES

Mary Simpson

1 box cake mix   30 flat-bottom ice cream cones

Prepare cake mix as directed. Pour scant ¼ c. into cones, filling ½ to ¾ full -- NO HIGHER. Bake about 30 minutes at 350 degrees.

FROSTING

2 egg whites   3 T. flour
1 cup Crisco   1 tsp. vanilla
2 cups powdered sugar

Frosting: (makes 2 batches) Beat egg whites stiff. Add Crisco and beat. Add sugar and beat. Add other ingredients and beat. Frost and decorate as desired. Mound frosting so it looks like top of ice cream cone.

Recipe Note: Great for kids to take to school for treat!

FORGOTTEN DESSERT

Carolyn Jack

6 egg whites   ½ tsp. cream of tartar
½ tsp. salt   1 cup sugar

Preheat oven to 475 degrees. In a large bowl beat egg whites until foamy. Add salt and cream of tartar. Add the 1 cup of sugar 1 tablespoon at a time. Beat for 15 minutes. Spread in an ungreased 9x9 pan. Turn off the oven and place pan in. Leave overnight. Do not open the oven until morning. Take out and spread with whipped topping and refrigerate. Serve with strawberries or fresh sliced peaches. Serves 9.

FRESH APPLE CAKE

Kathleen Dahl

2 cups chopped apples   1 egg
1 cup sugar   ½ tsp. salt
½ cup oil   1 cup chopped walnuts
1½ cups flour   1 tsp. baking soda

Combine all ingredients and put into a 9x13 inch pan. Bake at 350 degrees for 30 minutes or until knife inserted comes out clean. Serve warm with Cool Whip.

FRUIT COBBLER CAKE

Karen Churchill

3 eggs
1½ cups sugar
3 heaping T. shortening OR
6 T. oil

1½ c. milk
2 T. baking powder
5 Scoops flour
1 qt. fruit (any kind)

Mix all above ingredients except for fruit in a bowl. Put fruit in 13x9 pan. We like the three-berry frozen kind (raspberries, blackberries, and blueberries) or cherry, peaches or whatever fruit you have. Pour batter over fruit. Bake 350 degrees for 1 hour. Serves 8-10.

FRUIT COCKTAIL BARS

Marie Delio

2 eggs
1½ cups sugar
1 can undrained fruit cocktail
2¼ cup flour
1½ tsp. baking soda
½ tsp. salt
1 tsp. vanilla

1½ cup coconut
½ cup chopped nuts
½ cup butter
¾ cup sugar
¼ cup evaporated milk
½ cup nuts

Grease and flour jelly-roll pan. Beat eggs and 1½ cups sugar together. Then add fruit cocktail, flour, soda, salt, and vanilla. Spread in pan, top with nuts and coconut. Bake 25 minutes in a 350-degree oven. While that is baking combine butter, ¾ cup sugar, and evaporated milk together. Bring to a boil, cook 2 minutes. Spread on warm cake and top with nuts. Serve.

ICE CREAM DESSERT

Olivia Balczon

80 crushed Ritz crackers
2 sticks melted margarine or
  butter

2 boxes instant vanilla pudding
½ cup milk
½ gal. vanilla ice cream (softened)

Mix crushed crackers with margarine or butter and press into 9x13" pan. Bake at 350 degrees for 15 minutes. Cool. Mix pudding and milk together. Blend in soft ice cream. Pour onto cooled crust. Sprinkle with cracker crumbs and refrigerate at least 3 hours before serving.

Recipe Note: Can use chocolate ice cream and chocolate instant pudding also!

74987-06

ITALIAN LOVE CAKE

Eileen Kloecker Perino

1 chocolate cake mix
2 lbs. ricotta cheese
4 lg. eggs
3/4 cup sugar

1 tsp. vanilla
2 sm. instant chocolate pudding
2 cups milk
1 (12-oz.) Cool Whip

Prepare the chocolate cake and pour into greased and floured jelly-roll pan. DO NOT BAKE. Mix ricotta cheese, eggs, sugar, and vanilla. Pour over unbaked cake batter very slowly to completely cover cake mix. Bake 350 degrees for 35-45 minutes. Cool completely. When cake is cooled, mix 2 instant pudding mixes with 2 cups milk. Fold in Cool Whip. Frost cake and refrigerate.

Recipe Note: This feeds a crowd. Best made day ahead and refrigerate overnight.

MAN'S PIE

Carolyn Jack

1 cup graham cracker crumbs
1 cup white sugar
1 cup chopped nuts

1 tsp. baking powder
3 eggs

In a large bowl combine graham cracker crumbs, white sugar, chopped nuts, and baking powder. In a separate small bowl beat 3 egg yolks. Combine with the dry mixture. In another separate bowl beat 3 egg whites to soft peaks. Fold the whites into the other mixture. Place in a greased pie plate and bake for 25 minutes at 350 degrees. Serve with whipped topping or ice cream.

MEXICAN SUNDAE DESSERT

Mary Ann Yonko

FIRST LAYER

2 cups vanilla wafers, crushed   ½ cup margarine, melted
I cup Spanish peanuts, crushed

Mix above ingredients and bake 350 degrees for 8 to 10 minutes in a 9x13 pan.

SECOND LAYER

I (8-oz.) cream cheese, softened   I cup confectioners sugar
⅓ cup peanut butter   I carton Cool Whip, large

While first part is cooling, beat cream cheese, peanut butter, and sugar until smooth. Fold in with ½ the container Cool Whip. Spread on top of cooled first layer.

THIRD LAYER

2 pkgs. instant chocolate pudding,   3 cups milk
  small

Mix these ingredients until stiff. Mix with remaining Cool Whip. Top second layer.

TOPPING

crushed peanuts   shaved chocolate

Top. Chill and serve.

Erie
Times-News

MILE HIGH CHOCOLATE PIE

Kathleen Dahl

regular or graham cracker pie   2 small boxes chocolate instant
  shell   pudding mix
I pt. sour cream   Cool Whip
2 cups milk   chopped nuts (optional)

Mix sour cream, milk and chocolate pudding mix together. Spoon into crust. Chill. Top with Cool Whip and sprinkle with chopped nuts if desired.

74987-06

MOCHA-CHOCOLATE TRIFLE

Kathleen Findlay

1 (18.25 oz.) pkg. light devil's food
  cake mix
1-⅓ cups water
2 T. vegetable oil
2 large egg whites
1 large egg
cooking spray
3 cups cold, fat-free milk
1 (5.9 oz.) pkg. chocolate instant
  pudding mix

½ cup Kahlua (coffee-flavored
  liquor) or coffee (strong-brewed)
1 (8-oz.) carton frozen fat-free
  whipped topping, thawed
1 cup chopped, reduced-fat
  chocolate toffee bars (e.g. Heath
  Bars)

Preheat oven to 350 degrees. Combine first 5 ingredients in a large bowl. Beat at medium speed with a mixer until well-blended. Spoon batter onto a 13x9" baking pan, coated with cooking spray. Bake at 350 degrees for 35 minutes or until a wooden pick inserted in center comes out clean. Cool in pan for 10 minutes on a wire rack. Remove from pan. Cool completely on a wire rack. Combine milk and pudding mix in a medium bowl; prepare according to package directions. Tear half of cake into pieces; place in a 3-quart bowl or trifle dish. Pour half of Kahlua over cake pieces; top with half of pudding, whipped topping, and chocolate bars. Repeat procedure with remaining cake, Kahlua, pudding, whipped topping, and chocolate bars. Cover; chill at least 4 hours before serving. Yield: 16 servings, about 1 cup each.

Recipe Note: This spectacular dessert serves a crowd and can be made ahead of time!

MOM'S LEMON CREAM PIE

Betty Smulik

3 T. cornstarch
1 cup sugar
juice and zest of one lemon

¼ tsp. salt
2 cup milk
3 eggs

Combine sugar, cornstarch, salt and lemon zest. Add beaten egg yolks, mix well. Add milk a little at a time, heat to boiling. Boil gently until thick, add lemon juice and cook 1 minute. Pour into baked pie shell, cool, then cover, with meringue. Brown.

NO-BAKE FRUIT TART

Jennie Geisler
From the Erie Times–News

Erie
Times-News

1 reduced-fat graham cracker
  crust, prepared
1 (15-19-oz.) tub mascarpone or 8
  ounces light cream cheese
8 oz. frozen whipped topping (if
  using cream cheese)

¼ cup Splenda
juice from ½ a lemon
2 cups sliced fresh fruit in season
¼ cup sugar-free apricot
  preserves

If using light cream cheese, fold in whipped topping. Then, using a fork or mixer on low speed, gently combine softened cheese with Splenda and lemon juice. Spread into crust, gently, using a fork. Crumble the visible crust sides into a ring around the cheese mixture. Cover with sliced fruit. Mix preserves with a splash of water and microwave on high 30 seconds to liquify. Mix with a fork and continue microwaving until it resembles a shiny glaze. Brush glaze over fruit. Cover and chill at least 4 hours before slicing. Garnish with a sprig of mint. Serves 8.

Recipe Note: This is one of the sweetest ways to use fresh summer fruit in season. Per ⅛ pie made with mascarpone: 364 calories, 27 grams fat, 1.3 grams fiber, 6 grams protein, 27 grams carbohydrate, 339 milligrams sodium. Per ⅛ pie made with light cream cheese: 273 calories, 15 grams fat, 1.3 grams fiber, 5 grams protein, 32 grams carbohydrate, 269 milligrams sodium

NOCHTURES
(Coffee Cake)

Marjorie Hall

TOPPING

2 cups brown sugar
3 cups flour

1 cup oleo

Mix until crumbly. Take out 1½ cups for topping.

BASE

1 cup sour milk
2 eggs

1 tsp. salt
1 tsp. baking powder

Add to the remaining ingredients from topping. Place this mixture into a greased 9x13 pan and sprinkle topping all over. Sprinkle cinnamon and nutmeg on top. Bake for approx. 40 minutes at 350 degrees or until toothpick comes out clean.

74987-06

OLD-FASHIONED PINEAPPLE COOKIES

Sheila Coon

1 cup Domino sugar
2 eggs
1 stick margarine
1 tsp. pure vanilla

1 tsp. baking soda
1 cup crushed pineapple with juice
3 cups flour

Preheat oven to 350 degrees. Grease 2 cookie sheets with margarine. With electric mixer blend eggs, softened margarine, vanilla and baking soda. Add sugar till creamy then blend in crushed pineapple and juice. Add one cup of flour at time with mixer. The last cup of flour may need to be blended by hand as the dough is thick. Spoon onto greased cookie sheets and bake for approximately 8-10 minutes until a light golden brown. Cool on paper towels and store in cookie jar overnight.

Recipe Note: These cookies are best the next morning. Pineapple cookies say "welcome" in any language!

ORANGE DREAMSICLE CAKE

Holly Fleger

1 box vanilla cake mix
1 pkg. light Cool Whip
1 (8-oz.) pkg. light cream cheese, softened slightly
1 large can mandarin oranges, drained

1 T. vanilla extract
1 cup white chocolate chips
1 box instant orange Jell-O (sugar free)

Mix cake batter according to package directions. Once batter is done, mix in Jell-O powder. Then mix in white chocolate chips. Bake cake according to package directions in 2 (9-inch) round cake pans. Allow cake to cool. While cake is cooling, mix cream cheese, Cool Whip, and vanilla with electric mixer until fully mixed. Once cake is fully cooled, place 1 round cake on the serving platter, spread half of cream cheese icing on top, then top with half of mandarin oranges. Place other round cake on top of first, spread remaining cream cheese icing on top and top with remaining mandarin oranges. Refrigerate immediately and keep refrigerated until serving.

Recipe Note: Do not over-soften the cream cheese. If the cream cheese/Cool Whip mixture seems runny, refrigerate for a while before you spread it on the cake. You want the icing to stay in the layers and if it is too soft it will run down the sides of the cake.

OREO LAYERED DESSERT

Caroline Mulson

LAYER 1

1 pkg. Oreos, crushed   (Reserve ¾ cup)

LAYER 2

1 (8-oz.) pkg. cream cheese   1 (8-oz.) tub Cool Whip
1½ cup powdered sugar   1 tsp. vanilla

LAYER 3

2 pkgs. chocolate instant pudding   3 cups milk

LAYER 4

1 (8-oz.) tub Cool Whip   ¾ cup Oreos

Place crushed Oreos in 9x13 pan. Beat ingredients in Layer 2 together. Spread on top of crushed Oreos. Combine pudding and milk, beat 2 minutes. Spread on top of cream cheese layer. Add Cool Whip, top with crushed Oreos. Refrigerate.

PASSOVER BANANA CAKE

Eleanor Pless
Contributed by Rhonda Schember

12 eggs, separated   3 bananas, mashed
2 T. potato starch   ½ cup ground nuts
1½ cups cake meal   ⅛ tsp. salt
1¾ cups sugar

In large bowl, beat egg whites until stiff; set aside. In another large bowl, beat the yolks; gradually add sugar and salt, beating well. Add bananas and dry ingredients alternately to yolk mixture. Add nuts. Fold yolk mixture into beaten whites. Turn into a 10-inch ungreased tube pan lined with waxed paper. Bake in 325-degree oven for 1 hour. Invert and cool.

PEACH CUSTARD PIE

Sandy Case

1 (29-oz.) can peaches, drained
1 cup sugar, divided
3 T. cornstarch
3 T. reserved peach juice

1 stick margarine, melted
3 eggs
⅓ cup buttermilk
1 tsp. vanilla

Drain peaches, reserving 3 tablespoons syrup. Set aside. Cut peaches into small pieces. Place in a large bowl. Combine cornstarch and 2 to 3 tablespoons of the sugar. Add 3 tablespoons peach syrup and mix well. Add remaining sugar, eggs and buttermilk. Mix well. Stir in ½ cup melted margarine and vanilla. Pour over the peaches. Stir until peaches are coated. Pour filling into unbaked 10-inch pie crust. Cover with a top crust. Cut slits in the top to allow steam to escape. Brush with melted margarine and sprinkle with sugar. Bake at 400 degrees for 45 minutes in a 10-inch pie pan.

Recipe Note: Instead of buttermilk, you can measure 1 tsp. lemon juice in a cup and add enough milk to make it ⅓ cup.

PEANUT BRITTLE FRENCH TOAST

Esther Malaspina

1 loaf French sourdough bread
⅔ cup chunky peanut butter
⅔ cup butterscotch topping
½ cup whole milk
3 large eggs

1½ tsp. granulated sugar
½ tsp. vanilla extract
⅛ tsp. ground cinnamon
⅛ tsp. nutmeg
6 T. vegetable oil

Cut loaf of bread into two equal halves. Make a small slit in the crust of each half to create a pocket. Blend the peanut butter and the butterscotch. Now pipe in approximately 1 ounce of the blend into each pocket. Combine milk, eggs, sugar, vanilla, cinnamon and nutmeg. Dip both halves of the bread into this mixture, coating top and bottom. Fry in oil until golden brown. Serves 6

PEANUT BUTTER FUDGE

Carmella Berquist

2 cups sugar
⅔ cup milk
1 cup chunky peanut butter

1 tsp. vanilla
1 (16-oz.) jar marshmallow Fluff

Cook milk and sugar to soft ball stage. Add remaining ingredients. Mix well. Pour into buttered 9x9 pan.

Recipe Note: I found that if you boil milk and sugar for 7 minutes once it comes to a boil, it's long enough. If you double the recipe, boil it for about 10 minutes. Don't boil it too long or it will turn out sugary. This is just a hint if you don't know how to determine soft-ball stage.

PEANUT BUTTER PIE

Josephine Bandecca

⅔ cup creamy peanut butter
1 cup powdered sugar
1 (8-oz.) pkg. cream cheese

(8-oz.) Cool Whip
1 graham cracker pie shell

Erie
Times-News

Blend all ingredients together. Pour into pie shell. Spread remaining Cool Whip on top. Chill 3-4 hours.

Recipe Note: Suggestion: Try using Peter Pan Plus peanut butter.

PEANUT CRUNCH BARS

Maggie Link

1 saltine crackers to cover cookie sheet
1 (12-oz.) bag semi sweet chocolate chips

1 cup crushed peanuts
1 cup butter
1 cup packed brown sugar

Line cookie sheet with foil. Cover foil with saltine crackers so no foil shows through. Bring butter and brown sugar to a boil. Boil 2 minutes. Pour mixture over crackers so all are covered. Bake 350 degrees for 7 minutes. Cover with 1 bag chocolate chips put back in oven for 2 minutes. Spread chocolate over crackers top with peanuts. Chill in fridge. When hard break into small pieces.

PINEAPPLE CAKE

Arlene Spaulding

1 box yellow cake mix
1 can crushed pineapple, drained
1 tsp. vanilla
1 box vanilla instant pudding

1½ cups milk
1 (8-oz.) Cool Whip
shredded coconut

Prepare yellow cake mix according to the box and bake. Cool. Poke with fork every half inch all over. Spread pineapple evenly over cake. Make pudding according to directions on box. Spread pineapple over pudding and spread Cool Whip on top of that. Sprinkle with coconut.

74987-06

PINEAPPLE SHORTCAKE

Rosemary Repko

PART 1

3 T. cornstarch
½ cup brown sugar

½ cup sugar
2 large cans crushed pineapple

Stir above ingredients in heavy sauce pan. Cook over medium heat until thick. Let cool.

PART 2

4 cups flour
2 tsp. salt

1 cup Crisco

Sift flour and salt. Cut in Crisco with pastry blender. Set aside.

PART 3

2 eggs (beaten)
¾ cup sugar
1 cup sour cream

2 tsp. baking soda
2 tsp. vanilla

Mix above ingredients well. Add to flour mixture. Spread dough onto large cookie sheet. Place cooled pineapple mixture on top. Bake at 350 degrees for 30 minutes. When cooled, cut into bars and serve.

PUMPKIN BARS

Carmella Berquist

2 cups sugar
½ cup vegetable oil
1 (16-oz.) can pumpkin (2 cups)
4 eggs, beaten

2 cups Bisquick baking mix
2 tsp. cinnamon
½ cup raisins (optional)

Heat oven to 350 degrees. Grease jelly-roll pan (15½x10½ x1 inch). Beat sugar, oil, pumpkin and eggs on medium speed for one minute, scraping bowl occasionally. Stir in baking mix, cinnamon and raisins. Pour into pan. Bake 25 to 30 minutes or until toothpick inserted in center comes out clean. Cool. Frost with cream cheese frosting.

FROSTING

1 (3-oz.) pkg. cream cheese
⅓ cup oleo or butter
1 T. milk

1 tsp. vanilla
2 cups powdered sugar

Beat cream cheese, butter, milk and vanilla until creamy. Stir in powdered sugar until smooth.

PUMPKIN PIE

Helen Schember

1 single-crust pastry
¾ cup sugar
2 T. cornstarch, level
2 eggs
2 tsp. ground cinnamon

1 tsp. ground ginger
½ tsp. ground allspice (or cloves)
1 cup pumpkin
2 cups evaporated milk
dash salt

Prepare single-crust pastry; place in 9-inch pie shell and flute edges. Do not prick pastry. Beat together the sugar, salt, spices, cornstarch and eggs; add pumpkin and milk, stirring after each addition. Bake in a hot 450-degree oven for 10 minutes. Reduce heat to 325 degrees and bake another 30 minutes or until knife inserted in the center comes out clean.

PUMPKIN PIE

Bob Mix

1 cup granulated sugar
½ tsp. salt
1½ tsp. cinnamon
½ tsp. nutmeg
½ tsp. grated ginger
½ tsp. allspice

½ tsp. cloves
2 cups pumpkin, mashed
1 small can evaporated milk (or ¾ cup)
2 eggs

Mix the filling ingredients until smooth, then place in a 9-inch unbaked pie shell, and bake in a hot oven (400 degrees) for 15 minutes, then lower to moderate temperature (350 degrees) and continue baking for about 30 minutes or until custard is firm.

RASPBERRY-CREAM CHEESE COFFEE CAKE
Donna Donahue

1 (3-oz.) cream cheese
4 T. butter or oleo
2 cups packaged biscuit mix
⅓ cup milk

½ cup raspberry preserves
1 cup powdered sugar, sifted
1 to 2 T. milk
½ tsp. vanilla

Cut cream cheese and butter into biscuit mix until crumbly. Blend in ⅓ cup milk. Turn onto floured surface. Knead 8 to 10 strokes on wax paper. Roll dough to 12x 8-inch rectangle. Turn onto greased baking sheet, remove paper. Spread preserves down center of dough. Make 2½-inch cuts at 1-inch intervals on long sides. Fold strips over filling, slightly crossed. Bake 425 degrees for 12-15 minutes. Combine sugar, remaining milk and vanilla. Drizzle over top.

74987-06

RED CHOCOLATE CAKE

Marjorie Hall

CREAM TOGETHER:

½ cup oleo
1½ cups sugar

2 eggs

MAKE A PASTE OF:

(2-oz.) red food coloring

2 T. cocoa

Add paste to first mixture.

ADD TO:

2¼ cups flour
½ tsp. salt
1 tsp. vanilla

1 tsp. baking soda
2 T. vinegar

Add flour, salt and vanilla. Remove from mixer. Sprinkle baking soda and vinegar. Add remaining ingredients. Bake at 350 degrees for 40 to 45 minutes or until toothpick comes out clean.

REESE'S CUP CHEESECAKE

Holly Fleger

20 Oreo cookies
3 (8-oz.) pkgs. cream cheese, softened
⅓ cup butter/margarine, melted
1 (14-oz.) can sweetened condensed milk
1 cup chocolate syrup

2 tsp. vanilla extract
3 eggs, lightly beaten
30 Reese's cups (regular size) cut into fours
⅔ cup reduced fat creamy peanut butter, melted

Spray bottom and sides of a 9-inch springform pan with non-stick baking spray. Crush Oreo cookies (cream and all) into small pieces. In small bowl combine the cookie pieces and the melted butter/margarine. Press the cookie mixture into the bottom of the springform pan and bake at 325 degrees for 12 minutes. In a large bowl, beat the cream cheese, condensed milk and vanilla extract with an electric mixer until smooth. Mix in the chocolate syrup. Beat in the eggs. Stir in by hand ⅔ of the Reese's cup pieces (about 40 pieces) into the batter. Pour into the springform pan on top of crust. Bake at 325 degrees for 1 hour and 15 minutes until edges are pulling away from pan and the center is slightly set. Cool on counter for about a half hour. Top with remaining Reese's cup pieces. Pour melted peanut butter in between Reese's cup pieces to fill in gaps on top of cheesecake. Refrigerate immediately.

Recipe Note: It is very hard to judge when cheesecake is done baking because the center never really sets until it cools. You can judge best by the looks of the edge. Watch that it doesn't look overly brown.

RHUBARB CRUNCH

Kathleen Dahl

1 cup oleo, melted
2 cups flour
2 cups brown sugar
3 cups quick oatmeal
2 tsp. cinnamon
15 stalks rhubarb, cut into 1-inch
  pieces

2 cups white sugar
2 cups water
1 tsp. vanilla
2 T. cornstarch

Combine first 5 ingredients into crust-like mixture with a fork. Put about ½ of this mixture into a 9x13 inch pan. Cook sugar, water, vanilla, and cornstarch until clear. Place rhubarb on top of crust in pan and top with cooked sauce. Finish with remaining crust mixture. Bake for 1 hour at 300 degrees.

Recipe Note: Can be served with ice cream or whipped topping.

SNICKERS CAKE

Jeremiah Mulson

1 box chocolate cake mix (regular
  size)
1 stick butter
1 (14-oz.) bag caramels

⅓ cup milk
½ - 1 cup chopped nuts
(6-12 oz.) bag chocolate chips

Mix chocolate cake according to package directions. Pour half of the batter into a greased and floured 9x13 pan. Bake at 350 degrees for 20 minutes. While cake is baking, melt butter, caramels and milk. Stir until smooth. Pour over hot cake. Sprinkle nuts and chocolate chips over top. Pour remaining cake batter on top and spread gently, starting at edge and working in. Bake at 350 degrees for 20 minutes; reduce heat to 325 degrees and bake at 350 degrees for 20 minutes, reduce heat to 325 degrees and bake 10 minutes more.

74987-06

SOUR CREAM COFFEE CAKE

Karen Churchill

BATTER

1 stick margarine	2 cups flour
1 cup sugar	dash salt
2 eggs	1 tsp. baking soda
1 cup sour cream (I use fat free)	1 tsp. baking powder
6 T. milk	1 tsp. almond extract (I use more)
½ tsp. vanilla	

Cream margarine and sugar. Add eggs. Mix in remaining ingredients. Set aside.

TOPPING

½ cup sugar	½ cup chopped nuts
2 tsp. cinnamon	

Make topping with above ingredients. Grease and flour 11x7x2 pan. Layer ½ batter, ½ topping, ½ batter, ½ topping. Bake 350 degrees for 45 minutes. Serves 8-10.

STRAWBERRY PIZZA

Rosemary Repko

1 stick butter	¼ tsp. vanilla
1 cup self-rising flour	2 cups fresh strawberries
¼ cup powdered sugar	4 T. cornstarch
1 (8-oz.) pkg. cream cheese (softened)	1½ cups sugar
¼ tsp. lemon juice	1 (8-oz.) tub strawberry-flavored Cool Whip

Bring strawberries, cornstarch, and 1 cup of sugar to a boil in heavy sauce pan. Cook until thick. Cool and set aside. Mix butter, flour and powdered sugar. Spread onto round pizza pan. Bake at 325 degrees for 15 minutes or until lightly brown. Cool. Beat cream cheese, ½ cup sugar, lemon juice and vanilla until fluffy. Spread on cooled crust. Top with strawberry mixture. Spread Cool Whip on top of strawberries.

Recipe Note: I found this recipe in a Myrtle Beach newspaper.

SWEDISH BROWNIES

Olivia Balczon

Erie
Times-News

2 cups sugar
4 T. cocoa (rounded)
½ lb. margarine or butter (2 sticks)

1½ cups flour
2 tsp. vanilla
4 eggs

Melt margarine or butter, add remaining ingredients and mix well. Pour into greased 9x13 pan. Bake at 350 degrees for about 20-25 minutes.

Recipe Note: Doesn't need frosting!

SWEET POTATO PIE

Katherine Cole
Contributed by Rhonda Schember

2 cups hot, cooked sweet potatoes
1 cup sugar
¾ cup evaporated milk
6 T. butter

1 tsp. lemon juice
2 eggs
1 9-inch pie shell, baked and cooled

Combine sugar, sweet potatoes and butter. Mix by hand. Add lemon juice. Add eggs one at a time and beat with a hand mixer for 5 minutes after each addition. Add milk and blend on low speed for 5 minutes. Pour into pie shell. Bake in 325-degree oven for 1 hour or until knife inserted in center comes out clean.

74987-06

SWEET POTATO SPICE CAKE

Jennie Geisler
From the Erie Times–News

⅔ cup unbleached all-purpose flour
½ cup firmly packed light brown sugar
½ cup chopped, toasted pecans
⅛ tsp. salt
¼ cup unsalted butter, melted
¾ cup unsweetened applesauce
1½ cups firmly packed light brown sugar
3 large eggs

1 cup baked, mashed sweet potato, room temperature
1 T. molasses
1 T. finely grated fresh ginger
¾ tsp. salt
¼ tsp. ground cinnamon
¼ tsp. ground cardamom
¼ tsp. ground nutmeg
1⅔ cups all-purpose flour
1½ tsp. baking soda

In a small bowl, stir flour, brown sugar, pecans and salt. Drizzle melted butter over the dry ingredients and stir until well combined. The topping should not feel sandy. Add more melted butter if necessary. Position a rack in the center of the oven and preheat to 350 degrees. In a medium bowl, combine oil, brown sugar and eggs. Using a whisk, stir until mixture is smooth and sugar begins to dissolve, 30 to 60 seconds. If the sugar forms lumps, break them up with your fingers. A few tiny lumps are fine. Whisk in the sweet potato, molasses, ginger, salt and spices. Sift flour and baking soda together directly onto the batter. Use a whisk or rubber spatula to combine the ingredients until they are almost smooth. Pour batter into the prepared pan, spreading it evenly with a spatula. Sprinkle topping evenly over top. Bake 50 minutes, or until a wooden skewer comes out clean. Set the pan on a rack to cool 15 minutes. Run a knife around the edge of the pan. Let cool until just warm and cut into squares. Serve from the pan, or wrap well in plastic. Store at room temperature for up to one week. Serves 16.

Recipe Note: This is fun to make because no one can ever guess sweet potatoes are the secret ingredient. It's delicious with a cup of coffee any time of day. Per serving: 251 calories, 6.5 grams fat, ½ grams fiber, 3.7 grams protein, 45 grams carbohydrate, 279 milligrams sodium

WHITE CAKE "STRAWBERRY SUPREME"

Milton H. Murray

1 box white cake mix
1 box strawberry Jell-O

1 large Cool Whip
1 heaping qt. fresh strawberries

Erie
Times-News

First, make the white cake as per instructions on the package. When it is done, take it out of the oven and cool for one hour. About 20 minutes before the cake is cooled down, make the strawberry Jell-O mixture per instructions, but leave in a liquid state and "DO NOT" cool. When the cake has cooled, using a ½-inch dowel or similar circular item, place holes in the cake approximately 2½ inches apart over the entire cake area. Now, using a turkey baster, or somewhat similar utensil, fill the baster with the Jell-O mixture and then fill the holes in the cake to the level of the top of the cake. Only do this once or you will oversoak the cake. Once this is done, put a ½-inch layer of Cool Whip all over the surface of the cake. Slice the strawberries about ⅛-inch thick and cover the entire area of the Cool Whip. Place in refrigerator for at least 45 minutes. You're done.

Recipe Note: Just great tasting dessert for your family and guests. Bon Appetit.

74987-06

WHITE CHOCOLATE FRUIT TART

Jane (Rohleder) Voltz

¾ cup butter, or margarine, softened
½ cup confectioners' sugar
1½ cups all- purpose flour
1 (10-oz.) bag white chocolate chips, melted
¼ cup whipping cream
1 (8-oz.) pkg. cream cheese, softened

1 (20-oz.) can pineapple chunks
1 (11-oz.) can mandarin oranges, drained
2 kiwi fruit, peeled and sliced
3 T. sugar
2 tsp. cornstarch
½ tsp. lemon juice
½ cup reserved pineapple juice
Strawberries

In a small mixing bowl, cream butter and confectioners' sugar. Gradually add flour; mix well. Press into an ungreased 11-inch tart pan or 12-inch pizza pan with sides. Bake at 300 degrees for 25-30 minutes or until lightly browned. Cool. In a mixing bowl, beat the melted white chocolate chips and cream. Add cream cheese; beat until smooth. Spread over crust. Chill for 30 minutes. Drain pineapple, reserving ½ cup juice; set juice aside. Arrange pineapple, strawberries, oranges and kiwi in a pretty pattern over filling.

GLAZE

3 T. sugar
2 tsp. cornstarch

½ tsp. lemon juice
½ cup reserved pineapple juice

Combine sugar, cornstarch, lemon juice and reserved pineapple juice until smooth in a saucepan; bring to a boil over medium heat. Cook and stir for 2 minutes or until thickened. Refrigerate.

Recipe Favorites

Erie
Times-News

COOKIES & CANDY

BAKER'S WHITE CHOCOLATE COOKIES

Mandy Barney

2-lb. white chocolate chips
1 cup chunky peanut butter
2 cups Rice Krispies

2 cups dry roasted unsalted
  peanuts
2 cups mini marshmallows

Melt white chocolate in microwave or double boiler. Pour melted white chocolate over all ingredients in a bowl. Mix all ingredients together and drop by spoonfuls on wax paper. Let set 1 hour. Makes approx. 60 cookies.

BEST FUDGE IN THE WORLD

Tami Carrara
LaRue Nicholson
Paul Hogan – "master fudge maker"

2 cups milk
6 T. margarine
4 cups sugar
6 oz. marshmallows

1 tsp. vanilla
1½ cups peanut butter
1 (12-oz.) pkg. chocolate bits

Boil milk, margarine and sugar to 234 degrees on a candy thermometer. Remove from heat. Stir in the rest of the ingredients until melted. Pour into 4 - 1# candy boxes. Let sit until hard. Pour very large glass of milk and eat!

Recipe Note: Paul Hogan was a wonderful family friend. Every holiday he would bring us his peanut butter fudge and I would sneak to eat it. Thirty years later my mother, LaRue Nicholson, found Paul's recipe in with some papers she was cleaning out. Now, I make it for my son Giovanni to give to his teachers for a yummy holiday treat. Every one that I make it for begs me for the recipe!

BISCOTTI

Eileen Kloecker Perino
Tony Perino

Erie
Times-News

3 large eggs
1 cup sugar
3 cups flour
3 tsp. baking powder

2 tsp. anise seed
2 tsp. anise oil
1 cup slivered almonds (optional)
1 stick margarine

Set aside in a bowl: the flour and baking powder. Melt and cool margarine. Beat eggs in mixer, add sugar gradually, then cooled margarine slowly. Into the egg mixture add the anise seed and anise oil. Next add dry ingredients. This dough should be stiff, somewhat dry, not sticky. You may add more flour to obtain this texture. Finally, add almonds, if you choose. Divide dough into 4 parts. Form each part into a log, two logs to a greased or sprayed cookie sheet With floured hands flatten logs so the top is rounded to an arch. Bake at 350 degrees until set; they will not be browned. This takes 15-20 minutes. Pull out of oven and slice each log diagonally and turn slices on their sides. Bake till browned, flip each slice over and bake other side till browned. Cool and store in plastic bags. This is a coffee cookie. They should be hard when cooled.

CHOCOLATE BUTTERSCOTCH COOKIES

JoAnn Nagle

⅔ cup shortening
⅔ cup butter, softened
1 cup granulated sugar
1 cup brown sugar packed
2 eggs
3 tsp. vanilla

3 cups all-purpose flour
1 tsp. soda
1¼ tsp. salt
1½ cups chopped walnuts
6 oz. milk chocolate chips
6 oz. butterscotch chips

Heat oven to 375 degrees. Mix thoroughly shortening, butter, sugars, eggs and vanilla. Stir in remaining ingredients. If you want a softer, rounder cookie, add ½ cup more flour. Drop dough by rounded teaspoonfuls 2 inches apart on ungreased baking sheet. Bake 8-10 minutes until light brown. Cool slightly before removing from baking sheet. Makes about 7 dozen cookies.

CHOCOLATE DROP COOKIES

Marjorie Hall

4 cups brown sugar
4 eggs
2 cups oleo
2 tsp. baking soda
2 tsp. baking powder
2 cups milk

1½ cups cocoa
2 tsp. vanilla
6 cups flour
2 tsp. salt
2 cups chopped nuts

Mix well. Bake at 375 degrees. Makes 7 dozen.

74987-06

CHOCOLATE PIZZELLES

Dolores Wood
Contributed by Rhonda Schember

½ lb. butter, melted
1¾ cups sugar
6 eggs
1 tsp. almond flavoring
1 tsp. chocolate flavoring (from
   pharmacy)

½ tsp. salt
3 to 4 cups flour
1½ tsp. baking powder
2 T. cocoa

Melt the butter and cool a bit. Add sugar and beaten eggs, then gradually stir in flavorings. Combine flour, salt, baking powder and cocoa; add the egg mixture. Slowly mix to form dough mixture. Shape dough into small ball; place in center of pizzelle iron and close lid to bake. When cooked, carefully remove cookie to wire rack to cool.

COOKIES WITH PECANS AND CANDIED CHERRIES

Mary Smith

1 cup butter, no substitutes
1 cup sifted powdered sugar
1 egg
1 tsp. vanilla

2¼ cups sifted flour
1 cup chopped pecans
2 cups candied red cherries,
   chopped

Blend butter and powdered sugar. Add the egg and vanilla. Add the flour. Add the pecans and cherries. Chill for one hour. Divide the dough into 3 sections and make logs and roll in waxed paper. Chill for at least 3 hours. Cut the dough into ⅛- to ¼-inch slices. Bake on ungreased cookie sheet. Bake at 325 degrees about 13-15 minutes. Makes about 7 dozen cookies.

CORN FLAKE TREATS

Mandy Barney

1 cup sugar
1 cup white Karo syrup

1 cup creamy peanut butter
6 cups corn flakes

Bring sugar, Karo syrup and peanut butter to a boil. Don't overcook. Remove from stove and add 6 cups corn flakes. Press into buttered 9x13 pan. Cool, cut & eat!

EASTER EGGS

Nancy Phillips
Annamae Phillips

Erie
Times-News

½ cup butter or oleo
2 pkgs. vanilla pudding, small size,
  not instant
½ cup milk
1-lb. pkg. confectioners' sugar

1½ tsp. vanilla
½ cup peanut butter
walnuts
coconut

Melt butter/oleo. Mix in 2 packages pudding. Mix well; add milk and boil gently for 2 minutes, stirring constantly. Remove from heat. Add sugar and vanilla. For your choice of ½ cup peanut butter, walnuts or coconut. Stir until smooth. Shape into eggs when chilled. Cover with melted chocolate (I use semi-sweet chocolate chips) with a small amount of paraffin wax to hold.

EGG NOG DOODLES
(Like Snickerdoodles, but better!)

Cindy Hickernell

½ cup canola oil
½ cup sugar
1 egg
1 tsp. rum extract
1 tsp. vanilla extract

1⅓ cups flour
1 tsp. baking powder
½ tsp. nutmeg
⅛ tsp. salt (optional)
cinnamon sugar

Mix together oil and sugar. Beat in egg and extracts. Combine dry ingredients and add to mixture. Roll into 1-inch balls and roll in cinnamon sugar. Place on ungreased cookie sheets and bake at 375 degrees for 10 to 12 minutes. Remove immediately to cool on wire racks.

ERIE TIMES-NEWS FUDGE

*Beverly Whiting
Shirley Skadhauge*

18 oz. semi-sweet chocolate chips
1 can Eagle Brand milk
1 tsp. pure vanilla extract

1 dash salt
walnuts if you wish (opt.)

In saucepan, melt together all ingredients except walnuts over low heat. Add walnuts if you wish, and spread mixture in waxed-paper lined pan. Chill in refrigerator and cut into squares. Enjoy!

Recipe Note: This is an easy and delicious recipe, plus no cleanup. You may prefer to use 14 oz. chocolate chips and 4 oz. peanut butter chips. I prefer the chocolate/peanut butter chip mix myself. That's up to you. This recipe was given to me by a retiree from the Erie Times-News about 20 years ago and is in my "Keeper" file. I hope you enjoy it for as long as I have!

FANTASY FUDGE

Rhonda Schember

3 cups sugar
¾ cup butter
1 (5⅓-oz.) can evaporated milk (⅔ cup)
1 (12-oz.) bag semi-sweet chocolate pieces

1 (7-oz.) jar marshmallow creme
1 tsp. vanilla
1 cup chopped nuts

Combine sugar, butter and milk in 2-quart glass bowl or measuring cup. Microwave on HIGH, uncovered, 4½ - 5 minutes or until mixture starts to boil, stirring once. Microwave on HIGH an additional 5 minutes; stir in chocolate pieces until smooth. Blend in marshmallow creme and vanilla; stir in nuts. Pour into greased 12x8-inch dish or pan. Cool.

Recipe Note: Variation: add ¼ cup smooth peanut butter.

FIG COOKIES

Josephine Newara
Contributed by Rhonda Schember

FILLING

2 lbs. figs
1 lb. dates
1 cup raisins
1 orange
1 cup toasted almonds

1 tsp. cinnamon
1 large chocolate bar with almonds
1 cup honey
4 T. wine

Grind figs, dates, raisins, orange, almonds and cinnamon together. Place mixture in a large bowl and add chocolate bar (broken into small pieces), honey and wine; set aside.

DOUGH

5 cups flour
¾ cup sugar
½ tsp. salt
4 tsp. baking powder

1 cup solid shortening
2 tsp. vanilla
3 eggs
¾ - 1 cup milk

Cream shortening and sugar together. Add eggs and vanilla. Combine dry ingredients and add alternately with enough milk until dough no longer sticks to hands. Roll dough out onto floured board to ⅛-inch thickness. Cut into 12x3-inch strips. Place filling in the center of each strip. Fold one side over and lightly pat or seal. Then fold completely over so seam is on the bottom. Bake on ungreased cookie sheet at 400 degrees until lightly browned. Makes 10 dozen.

FROSTED BANANA BARS

Jacque Mulson

Erie
Times-News

½ cup butter or margarine,
  softened
2 cups sugar
3 eggs
1½ cups mashed ripe bananas
  (about 3 medium)

1 tsp. vanilla extract
2 cups all-purpose flour
1 tsp. baking soda
pinch salt

In a mixing bowl, cream butter and sugar. Beat in eggs, bananas and vanilla. Combine the flour, baking soda and salt; add to creamed mixture and mix well. Pour into a greased 15x10x1 baking pan. Bake at 350 degrees for 25 minutes or until bars test done. Cool.

FROSTING

½ cup cutter or margarine,
  softened
1 (8-oz.) pkg. cream cheese,
  softened

4 cups confectioners' sugar
2 tsp. vanilla extract

Cream butter and cream cheese in a mixing bowl. Gradually add confectioners' sugar and vanilla; beat well. Spread over bars.

Recipe Note: Yield: 3 dozen

GARBAGE

Betty Smulik

1 2-lb. bag white chocolate wafers
1 small bag pretzels

1 can mixed nuts
5 cups Cheerios or Chex cereal

Melt chocolate on low in double boiler. In large bowl mix dry ingredients. Pour chocolate over mixture and stir until coated. Spread onto foil covered cookie sheets and refrigerate until hard. Break into chunks and store in zippered plastic bags.

Recipe Note: It may be difficult to break into chunks. If this is encountered try using a serrated knife to cut into chunks.

74987-06

HEAVENLY CINNAMON STAR COOKIES

Peach McVey

6 large egg whites
2 tsp. cinnamon
4 cups confectioners' sugar

1 tsp. grated lemon peel
4 cups ground blanched almonds
(1 pound)

Heat oven to 350 degrees. Beat egg whites until stiff but not dry. Gradually stir in confectioners' sugar. Spoon out about 1¾ cups for frosting stars. Set aside. To the rest of the mixture, blend in ground almonds, cinnamon, lemon peel and 1 cup more of the powdered sugar. Refrigerate until the dough is workable. On waxes paper dusted with powdered sugar, put ⅓ of the dough. Add some sugar and roll until ⅛-inch thick. Cut with 2¾-inch star cutter. Place on cookie sheet lined with parchment paper. Bake 10 minutes. Cook and frost with reserved meringue. Return to 325-degree oven for 5 minutes.

Recipe Note: I won $100 in the Erie Times-News cookie contest for this recipe about 15 years ago.

HONEY EVERYDAY COOKIES

Donna Strong

½ cup shortening
½ cup sugar
½ cup honey
1 egg
⅔ cup flour
½ tsp. soda

½ tsp. baking powder
¼ tsp. salt
1 cup quick cooking oats
1 cup shredded coconut
1 tsp. vanilla
½ cup chopped nuts

Cream shortening, sugar and honey together. Add well-beaten egg. Sift flour with dry ingredients. Stir well. Add oats, coconut, vanilla and nuts. Spread on greased cookie sheet. Do not overcook. Bake 12-15 min. 350 degrees Cut into bars. These bars are healthy eating.

KILLER CHOCOLATE CHIP COOKIES

Sandy Reid
Mike Orsini
Mercyhurst Prep class of '07

Erie
Times-News

³/₄ cup Crisco, butter-flavored
1¼ cups firmly packed light
  brown sugar
2 T. milk
1 T. pure vanilla extract
1 large egg
1³/₄ cups all-purpose flour
1 tsp. salt

³/₄ tsp. baking soda
³/₄ cup semi-sweet chocolate chips
  or mini chips
³/₄ cup semi-sweet chocolate
  chunks
1 cup pecans or walnuts coarsely
  chopped

Combine Crisco, brown sugar, milk and vanilla in a large bowl. Beat at medium speed of electric mixer until well blended. Beat egg into creamed mixture. Combine flour, salt, and baking soda. Mix into creamed mixture just until blended. Stir in chocolate chips and pecan pieces. Drop by rounded tablespoonful 3 inches apart onto an ungreased baking sheet. Bake one baking sheet at a time at 375 degrees for 8 to 10 minutes for chewy cookies. Cookies will appear moist - do not over bake OR 11 to 13 minutes for crisp cookies. Cool 2 minutes on the baking sheet. Complete cooling on wire racks. Then take them to the theater rehearsals at Mercyhurst and watch them disappear!

LEMON BARS

Mary Perry

CRUST

1 cup all-purpose flour
¹/₃ cup butter or margarine
  (softened)

¼ cup confectioners' sugar

TOPPING

1 cup sugar
2 eggs
2 T. all-purpose flour
2 T. lemon juice (squeezed)

½ tsp. lemon extract
½ tsp. baking powder
¼ tsp. salt
confectioners' sugar

Combine crust ingredients and put into an 8-inch square pan. Bake at 375 degrees for 15 minutes. Meanwhile, combine sugar, eggs, flour, lemon juice, extract, baking powder and salt in a mixing bowl. Mix until frothy, pour over cooled crust. Bake at 375 degrees for 18-22 minutes or until light-golden brown. Cool and dust with confectioners' sugar (sifted).

74987-06

OATMEAL CRISPIES COOKIES

Kathleen Dahl

1 cup Crisco
1 cup white sugar
1 cup brown sugar
2 eggs
1 tsp. vanilla
3 cups quick oats

1½ cups all-purpose flour
1 tsp. salt
1 tsp. baking soda
¼ tsp. cinnamon
¼ tsp. ground nutmeg
raisins, to individual preference

Cream shortening and sugar. Add eggs one at a time. Beat in vanilla. Combine remaining ingredients in a separate bowl. Gradually add to creamed mixture. Drop by teaspoonfuls 2 inches apart on ungreased cookie sheets. Flatten with fork lightly. Bake at 350 degrees 10-12 minutes.

OATMEAL, CHOCOLATE CHIP, PEANUT BUTTER COOKIES

Jeanne Johannesmeyer

½ cup white sugar
½ cup soft margarine
½ cup peanut butter (chunky)

½ tsp. vanilla
1 egg

Mix above together in large bowl until creamy.

1 cup flour
1 tsp. baking soda
⅓ cup confectioners' sugar

½ cup quick oats
¼ tsp. salt
(6-oz.) mini-chocolate chips

Mix above ingredients together. Add to above ingredients, then stir in 6 ounces mini-chocolate chips. Drop onto cookie sheet (ungreased). Once baked, cool 1 minute before taking off cookie sheet. Bake 350 degrees for 9-12 minutes. Makes 3 dozen cookies.

Recipe Note: Great with a glass of milk!

ORANGE DROP COOKIES

Marjorie Hall
Mom's Recipe

3 cups brown sugar
2 cups oleo
4 eggs
1 cup sour milk
2 tsp. baking soda

4 tsp. baking powder
7 to 8 cups flour
2 grated rinds of 2 oranges and
  juice

Combine all ingredients. Drop onto cookie sheet and bake at 375 degrees. Makes about 7 dozen.

PAYDAY CANDY

Barbara Valaitis

6 cups Rice Chex cereal
1 cup white sugar
1 cup peanut butter (smooth or
chunky)

2 cups peanuts (if using smooth
peanut butter)
1 cup Karo syrup
1 tsp. vanilla

Over medium heat, in a large pot, stir together white sugar and Karo syrup until it boils. Boil 1 minute without stirring. Add vanilla and peanut butter. Stir over medium heat until the peanut butter melts. Stir in Chex and peanuts. Pour onto cookie sheet in a thin layer. Let cool. Break into pieces.

PEANUT BUTTER COOKIES

Mary Smith

1 cup lard or vegetable shortening
1 cup light brown sugar
1 cup white sugar
1 cup peanut butter
2 eggs, well beaten

1 tsp. vanilla
3 cups sifted flour
2 tsp. baking soda
1 tsp. salt
1½ T. milk

Mix ingredients in order given. Cream the shortening, brown sugar, and white sugar. Add the peanut butter and vanilla. Add the 2 eggs. Add the flour, baking soda, and salt. Roll into balls about 1 inch in diameter. Place on ungreased cookie sheet. Press with fork. Bake at 350 degrees for 10-12 minutes or until light brown.

Note: Add milk and watch adding flour. Do not make the dough too stiff.

Recipe Note: This recipe is over 70 years old. It was given to my mother by a neighbor who was born in Sweden.

74987-06

PECAN FROSTIES

Maureen Bemko

2 cups flour
½ tsp. baking soda
¼ tsp. salt
½ cup sweet cream butter, softened
1 cup brown sugar, packed

1 tsp. vanilla extract
1 egg
1 cup pecans, chopped
½ cup brown sugar, packed
¼ cup sour cream

Sift flour with baking soda and salt. In a large bowl, cream butter and 1 cup brown sugar. Beat in vanilla and egg. Gradually add dry ingredients. Chill bowl briefly until dough can be shaped into 1-inch balls. Place balls 2 inches apart on ungreased cookie sheet. Make a depression in the center of each ball. Combine pecans, ½ cup brown sugar, and sour cream in small bowl. Place 1 teaspoonful of the pecan topping in each depression. Bake at 350 degrees for about 12 minutes.

Recipe Note: This fabulous Pillsbury Bake-Off-winning recipe comes with two caveats: Don't substitute margarine or low-fat sour cream (the results are disappointing), and when I brought these to a function one time I swear I heard a man call them "those ugly cookies." He would've eaten his words had he eaten these cookies!

PICTURE PERFECT BROWNIES

Loretta Grumblatt
Contributed by Rhonda Schember

½ cup solid shortening
1 cup sugar
4 eggs
1 tsp. vanilla
1 (16-oz.) can chocolate-flavored syrup

1¼ cups sifted flour
½ tsp. salt
1 cup chopped walnuts, optional
nonstick vegetable spray

Cream together shortening and sugar; beat in eggs and vanilla. Slowly add in syrup, flour, salt and walnuts, if desired. Spread batter into a 9x13x2-inch baking pan sprayed with nonstick vegetable coating. Bake in 350 degree oven for 30-35 minutes. Cool brownies 5 minutes, then top with frosting.

FROSTING

⅔ cup sugar
3 T. milk
2 T. solid shortening

¼ tsp. salt
½ cup semi-sweet chocolate pieces
½ tsp. vanilla extract

Bring sugar, milk, shortening and salt to a boil and boil for 30 seconds. Remove from heat and stir in semi-sweet chocolate pieces and vanilla. Cool 10 minutes; spread over brownies.

SNOWFLAKE MACAROONS

Arlene Spaulding

2²⁄₃ cups Baker's coconut
²⁄₃ cup sugar
6 T. flour

¼ tsp. salt
4 egg whites
1 tsp. almond extract

Erie
Times-News

Preheat oven to 325 degrees. Lightly grease and flour cookie sheet. Mix coconut, sugar, flour and salt in a bowl. Stir in egg whites and almond extract until well blended. Drop by teaspoonfuls onto cookie sheet. Bake for 20 minutes or until edge of cookies are a golden brown.

STEPH'S DISGUSTINGLY RICH BROWNIES

Stephanie Reid
My good ol' Dad

2 cups sugar
4 eggs
³⁄₄ cup Hershey's cocoa
1¼ cups all-purpose flour
¼ tsp. salt

1 tsp. vanilla extract
2 sticks butter
½ cup chopped walnuts, optional
shortening to grease the pan

Preheat oven to 350 degrees, then grease the inside of an 8x9-inch baking pan with shortening. Melt the butter over a low heat or in the microwave just until melted. In a mixing bowl, stir the cocoa and sugar together. Then stir in the butter. Add the eggs and vanilla and stir again. Now add the flour and salt, and mix just until smooth. If you are using walnuts, now is the time to add them. Scrape the mixture out into the greased pan and spread out in an even layer. Bake in a 350-degree oven until the brownies just begin to pull away from the sides of the pan or until you can stick a toothpick in and pull it out with no batter sticking to it. This takes about 40 to 50 minutes to bake. Let cool before cutting into generous squares.

Recipe Note: These brownies are wonderful under a nice scoop of ice cream. Yummm!

SURE-BET MACAROONS

Pat Rhone

1 pt. orange sherbet
1 pkg. Pillsbury white cake mix

1½ T. almond extract
6 cups Baker's coconut

Soften sherbet in large bowl. Add cake mix and almond extract, blend just until well mixed. Stir in coconut. Drop by round teaspoonfuls onto greased cookie sheets. Bake at 350 degrees for 10-13 minutes or until light brown. Makes about 72 cookies.

Recipe Note: For variety, different flavors of sherbet may be used.

74987-06

SWEDISH SUGAR COOKIE

Mary Simpson

COOKIE

1 cup sugar	2 cups flour
1 cup shortening	½ tsp. cream of tartar
1 egg	½ tsp. baking soda
½ tsp. vanilla	½ tsp. salt

Cream sugar and shortening. Add egg, vanilla. Add dry ingredients. Make pieces of dough the size of walnuts. Press down with fork dipped in water. (Dough is sort of hard.) Bake at 375 degrees for 10 minutes.

FROSTING

¼ cup margarine	1 tsp. vanilla
2 cups sugar	milk, as needed
⅛ tsp. salt	

Combine. Add milk to get desired consistency.

TOFFEE

Sherry Rieder

1 lb. butter (salted)	1 oz. rum
2¼ cups sugar	2 cups chopped peanuts (divided)
1 T. vanilla	7-8 Hershey chocolate bars

Combine first four ingredients in large pot and cook over high-ish heat, stirring constantly until mixture becomes caramel color. (This will take 20 to 25 minutes, or so.) Do not use a plastic spoon, because it will melt. When it's caramel color, turn off the heat and quickly stir in 1 cup chopped peanuts. Spread quickly into buttered cookie sheet. (Butter the cookie sheet before you start this process, because there will be no time to do it midway through.) Top with Hershey chocolate bars. Heat will melt the chocolate. Smooth it with spatula and top with 1 cup chopped nuts. Cool and break into pieces.

Recipe Note: Do not stop cooking until it's caramel/peanut butter color. It's almost burning (smoking) when it's done.

WHOOPIE PIES
(Chocolate Gobbles)

Donna Donahue

½ cup oil
1 cup sugar
1 tsp. vanilla
1 egg
1 cup milk

½ tsp. baking powder
½ tsp. salt
2 cups flour
1½ tsp. baking soda
½ cup cocoa

Combine oil, sugar, egg, milk and vanilla. Add to dry ingredients. Drop by teaspoon onto ungreased cookie sheet. Flatten slightly. Bake 400 degrees for 3 to 4 minutes.

FILLING

1½ cups Crisco
2½ cups confectioners' sugar
2 egg whites, unbeaten

2 tsp. vanilla
4 T. flour

Cream Crisco and confectioners' sugar. Add other ingredients. Beat until fluffy. Spread filling on one cookie and top with second cookie. Sprinkle confectionary sugar over them.

Recipe Favorites

74987-06

THIS & THAT

ALMOND CREAM STRAWBERRIES

Virginia Rotthoff
Contributed by Rhonda Schember

2 pints large, fresh strawberries
1 small box instant vanilla pudding
1 cup milk

1 tsp. almond extract
½ pint whipping cream, whipped

Cut a deep "X" into the top of each berry; spread apart. Prepare pudding with 1 cup milk; gently fold whipped cream and almond extract into the pudding. Pipe the cream into each berry with a pastry bag.

APPLE DIP

Pat Thunborg
Contributed by Rhonda Schember

1 (8-oz.) pkg. cream cheese,
  softened
¼ cup brown sugar, packed
4 tsp. lemon juice
½ tsp. lemon peel, grated

¼ tsp. ground nutmeg
¼ tsp. ground cinnamon
red, yellow and green, sliced
  apples

With a wire whisk, cream together the cream cheese and brown sugar. Add remaining ingredients and stir until smooth. Serve with sliced apples dipped in lemon juice to prevent browning.

AVOCADO-FETA SALSA

Mary Agnes Mosher

4 plum tomatoes, chopped
2 T. finely chopped red onion
2 cloves garlic, minced
1 (4-oz.) pkg. crumbled feta cheese
1 T. chopped fresh parsley
3 T. red wine vinegar

2 T. olive oil
½ tsp. dried oregano
½ tsp. salt
2 avocados, chopped
assorted tortilla chips

Mix everything together except chips.

Recipe Note: Make this salsa the day it will be served. Avoid refrigerating it as the texture of the tomatoes will soften.

CAREY FAMILY BARBECUE SAUCE

Mary G. Holman

Erie
Times-News

2 T. molasses
½ cup catsup
4 T. apple cider vinegar
3 T. salad oil (canola or corn)
4 T. water
1 pinch ground nutmeg
½ tsp. garlic powder

3 T. Worcestershire sauce
¼ tsp. salt
1 T. tomato paste
1 packed T. dark or light brown
  sugar
¼ tsp. Tabasco sauce

In a small saucepan, combine all the ingredients and blend thoroughly with a wire whisk. Bring to a boil, then lower heat and simmer, stirring occasionally for 3 minutes or until slightly thickened. Cool and store in the refrigerator in a glass jar.

Recipe Note: This was my mother's recipe, which we all used for oven roasting and outdoor cooking. It can be used both as a marinade or a sauce on chicken, pork or beef. Use ½ tsp. Tabasco for more heat.

CHOCOLATE CHIP CHEESE BALL

Jacque Mulson

1 (8-oz.) pkg. cream cheese,
  softened
½ cup butter, softened
¼ tsp. vanilla
¾ cubes mini morsel chocolate
  chips

¾ cup confectioners' sugar
2 T. brown sugar
¾ cup finely chopped pecans
graham crackers or chocolate
  crackers

In a mixing bowl, beat cream cheese, butter and vanilla until fluffy. Gradually add sugars and beat until just combined. Stir in chocolate chips. Cover and refrigerate for 2 hours. Place on plastic wrap and form into a ball. Refrigerate for another hour. Just before serving, roll cheese ball in pecans. Serve with graham crackers.

CREAM FROSTING

Marjorie Hall

1½ cup granulated sugar
½ cubes oleo (soft)
½ cup Crisco (soft)

1 egg white
⅔ cup milk (lukewarm)
1 tsp. vanilla

Beat the sugar, oleo and Crisco until fluffy. Add egg white, milk and vanilla. Beat for 15 or 20 minutes longer. Watch so milk is not hotter than lukewarm.

Recipe Note: Greatest of all frostings!

74987-06

EASY PIZZA SAUCE
(No Cook)

Mary Ann Yonko

1 can tomato purée (large)
1 can tomato sauce (small)
½ cup oil
2 heaping T. Parmesan cheese
1 tsp. sugar
1 tsp. salt
¼ tsp. pepper

2 T. oregano
1 T. parsley
2 tsp. crushed red pepper flakes
dash onion salt
dash garlic salt (or fresh if desired)
3 med. pizza shells

Mix and spread on pizza shells. Add favorite toppings. Bake. Covers 3 medium round shells.

FRENCH SALAD DRESSING

Donna Donahue

¾ cup vinegar
1 cup sugar
1 tsp. salt
1 tsp. pepper
1 tsp. paprika

1 T. prepared mustard
3 T. chopped onions
1 tsp. Worcestershire sauce
1½ cup salad oil
1 can tomato soup

Combine all ingredients with blender or shake vigorously.

GREEK SAUCE

Elaine Brady

1 lb. ground beef
1 (15-oz.) can tomato sauce
1 can water
1 tsp. basil
1 tsp. oregano
1 tsp. crushed red pepper
1 tsp. garlic salt

1 tsp. chili powder
½ to 1 tsp. salt
¼ to 1 tsp. cayenne pepper
1 T. French's mustard
1 tsp. cumin Must use!
2 medium onions, chopped

Fry and drain ground beef. Add other ingredients and simmer uncovered for 1½ to 2 hours.

LIGHT HUMMUS

Jennie Geisler
From the Erie Times–News

1 (15-19-oz.) can chickpeas, undrained
4 tsp. tahini
1 T. fresh lemon juice

1 tsp. grated lemon rind
1 clove garlic, chopped
⅛ tsp. ground cumin
⅛ tsp. salt

Drain chickpeas, reserving ⅓ cup of the canned liquid, set aside In a food processor or blender, combine the chickpeas, tahini, lemon juice, lemon rind, garlic, cumin and salt. With the processor running, gradually add the reserved liquid through the feed tub and process until smooth. Makes 1½ cups for 6¼-cup servings

Recipe Note: Store-bought hummus can really rack up the calories and fat. This is a light version from Weight Watchers "Take Out Tonight!" Per ¼ cup: 63 calories, 2 grams fat, 2 grams fiber, 3 grams protein, 8 grams carbohydrate, 192 milligrams sodium, 0 cholesterol, 23 milligrams calcium

MAYONNAISE

Bob Mix

3-4 cloves garlic
½ tsp. salt
1 T. prepared mustard
2 fresh, whole eggs

1 to 1½ fluid ounces fresh lemon juice
1½ cup vegetable oil (approx.)

Preparation: Peel and dice the garlic, adding the salt, mustard, lemon juice and whole eggs into the bowl of your blender, and blend at high speed for a full minute. Then, without turning off the blender, slowly add the vegetable oil through the opening in the cover of the blender, listening to the sound of the motor as the mixture is being beaten. When you perceive a sudden increase in speed of the blender knife, the mayonnaise is done. Stop the blender and empty the mayonnaise into a clean jar and store in the refrigerator. (Hint: It's easier emptying bowl through bottom) Emulsification: Is sometimes tricky, depends on several factors. It's important to have blended the premixture well before adding the oil, and to add the oil very slowly to assure successful emulsion. Should the mixture not emulsify: After the oil is added, just stop the blender and empty the contents into a clean bowl or other recipient. Then, without rinsing the blender, blend an additional egg and add the mixture. You will find that the lower portion will emulsify rapidly, but you'll need to stop the blender several times to insert a spatula to blend the entire contents before storage and use.

PINK PICKLED ONIONS

Donna Donahue

l cup sugar	2 tsp. salt
l cubes red wine vinegar	3 lbs. onions, sliced
¼ cup water	l tsp. pickling spices
l T. whole mustard seed	2 T. Grenadine syrup (optional)

Bring sugar, vinegar, water, mustard seed, salt and pickling spices to a boil in a large pot. Stir in onions, cover and simmer 5-7 minutes. Stir once or twice until crisp and tender. Remove from heat and stir in Grenadine. Pack onions and liquid in jars. Cool, cover and refrigerate. Makes 8 cups.

Recipe Note: Will store in refrigerator for 2 months.

SALSA

Heather Cass

4 cup tomatoes, chopped, drain juice	½ cup hot peppers, seeded & chopped
¾ cup onion, chopped	1½ tsp. salt
2 cup green peppers, seeded & chopped	½ cup white vinegar
	2 cloves garlic

Chop & seed peppers and tomatoes. Mix ingredients in a large stockpot & bring to a boil. Simmer for 20 minutes. To can, process 30 minutes in a hot water bath.

Recipe Note: I usually double this recipe and it makes enough to can eight pint-size jars.

SIMPLE TOMATO SAUCE

Marnie Mead Oberle

l stick butter	2 cups chicken broth, preferably homemade, otherwise buy organic
¼ cup olive oil	
2 cups onions, chopped	
2 cloves garlic, minced	salt
l (26-28 oz.) can tomatoes, crushed	

Melt butter and olive oil over medium heat. Add onions and sauté until translucent, about 10-15 minutes. Add garlic and cook until fragrant, about a minute. You do not want garlic to brown. Add tomatoes and chicken broth. Cook about 45 minutes over medium heat, or until you don't see any liquid separating from the tomatoes. Add salt to taste.

Recipe Note: This is my base for almost all sauce recipes. You can add sausage or meatballs for a hearty sauce, or you can add some heavy cream, vodka, some hot red pepper flakes and frozen peas for a vodka sauce. This also makes a nice base for lasagna.

THAI PEANUT SAUCE

Marnie Mead Oberle

½ cup creamy peanut butter
½ cup unsweetened coconut milk
2 T. fresh lime juice
½ cup soy sauce, preferably
  tamari

1 T. honey
1 T. chili and garlic sauce

Combine and refrigerate. Will keep for about 5 days.

Recipe Note: This is great tossed with rotisserie chicken from the supermarket, some cooked pasta (I like angel hair), and any veggie assortment you like. Drain pasta in a colander with frozen bell pepper strips, broccoli and sugar snap peas to cook the frozen veggies. Top with chopped cashews or peanuts for a nice presentation.

YOGCHSTRAWA

Terry Dollivar

1 large pkg. vanilla yogurt
½ cup cherries

½ cup strawberries
⅓ cup chopped walnuts

Combine all ingredients. Serve.

Recipe Favorites

Erie
Times-News

74987-06

INDEX OF RECIPES

VEGETABLES & SIDE DISHES

MAIN DISHES

BREADS & ROLLS

DESSERTS

COOKIES & CANDY

THIS & THAT

How to Order

Get additional copies of this cookbook by returning
an order form and your check or money order to:

Erie Times - News
205 West 12th Street
Erie, PA 16534
(814) 870-1697

Please send me _____ copies of **Cooking With ETN
and Friends** at **$19.95** per copy and $_____ for shipping
and handling per book. Enclosed is my check or money
order for $_____.

Mail Books To:

Name _____

Address _____

City _____ State _____ Zip _____

Please send me _____ copies of **Cooking With ETN
and Friends** at **$19.95** per copy and $_____ for shipping
and handling per book. Enclosed is my check or money
order for $_____.

Mail Books To:

Name _____

Address _____

City _____ State _____ Zip _____

Cooking Tips

1. After stewing a chicken, cool in broth before cutting into chunks; it will have twice the flavor.

2. To slice meat into thin strips, as for stir-fry dishes, partially freeze it so it will slice more easily.

3. A roast with the bone in will cook faster than a boneless roast. The bone carries the heat to the inside more quickly.

4. When making a roast, place dry onion soup mix in the bottom of your roaster pan. After removing the roast, add 1 can of mushroom soup and you will have a good brown gravy.

5. For a juicier hamburger, add cold water to the beef before grilling (½ cup to 1 pound of meat).

6. To freeze meatballs, place them on a cookie sheet until frozen. Place in plastic bags. They will stay separated so that you may remove as many as you want.

7. To keep cauliflower white while cooking, add a little milk to the water.

8. When boiling corn, add sugar to the water instead of salt. Salt will toughen the corn.

9. To ripen tomatoes, put them in a brown paper bag in a dark pantry, and they will ripen.

10. To keep celery crisp, stand it upright in a pitcher of cold, salted water and refrigerate.

11. When cooking cabbage, place a small tin cup or can half full of vinegar on the stove near the cabbage. It will absorb the odor.

12. Potatoes soaked in salt water for 20 minutes before baking will bake more rapidly.

13. Let raw potatoes stand in cold water for at least a half-hour before frying in order to improve the crispness of French-fried potatoes. Dry potatoes thoroughly before adding to oil.

14. Use greased muffin tins as molds when baking stuffed green peppers.

15. A few drops of lemon juice in the water will whiten boiled potatoes.

16. Buy mushrooms before they "open." When stems and caps are attached firmly, mushrooms are truly fresh.

17. Do not use metal bowls when mixing salads. Use wood, glass or china.

18. Lettuce keeps better if you store it in the refrigerator without washing it. Keep the leaves dry. Wash lettuce the day you are going to use it.

19. Do not use soda to keep vegetables green. It destroys Vitamin C.

20. Do not despair if you oversalt gravy. Stir in some instant mashed potatoes to repair the damage. Just add a little more liquid in order to offset the thickening.

Herbs & Spices

Acquaint yourself with herbs and spices. Add in small amounts, ¼ teaspoon for every 4 servings. Crush dried herbs or snip fresh ones before using. Use 3 times more fresh herbs if substituting fresh for dried.

Basil
Sweet, warm flavor with an aromatic odor. Use whole or ground. Good with lamb, fish, roast, stews, ground beef, vegetables, dressing and omelets.

Bay Leaves
Pungent flavor. Use whole leaf but remove before serving. Good in vegetable dishes, seafood, stews and pickles.

Caraway
Spicy taste and aromatic smell. Use in cakes, breads, soups, cheese and sauerkraut.

Chives
Sweet, mild flavor like that of onion. Excellent in salads, fish, soups and potatoes.

Cilantro
Use fresh. Excellent in salads, fish, chicken, rice, beans and Mexican dishes.

Curry Powder
Spices are combined to proper proportions to give a distinct flavor to meat, poultry, fish and vegetables.

Dill
Both seeds and leaves are flavorful. Leaves may be used as a garnish or cooked with fish, soup, dressings, potatoes and beans. Leaves or the whole plant may be used to flavor pickles.

Fennel
Sweet, hot flavor. Both seeds and leaves are used. Use in small quantities in pies and baked goods. Leaves can be boiled with fish.

Ginger
A pungent root, this aromatic spice is sold fresh, dried or ground. Use in pickles, preserves, cakes, cookies, soups and meat dishes.

Herbs & Spices

Marjoram May be used both dried or green. Use to flavor fish, poultry, omelets, lamb, stew, stuffing and tomato juice.

Mint Aromatic with a cool flavor. Excellent in beverages, fish, lamb, cheese, soup, peas, carrots, and fruit desserts.

Oregano Strong, aromatic odor. Use whole or ground in tomato juice, fish, eggs, pizza, omelets, chili, stew, gravy, poultry and vegetables.

Paprika A bright red pepper, this spice is used in meat, vegetables and soups or as a garnish for potatoes, salads or eggs.

Parsley Best when used fresh, but can be used dried as a garnish or as a seasoning. Try in fish, omelets, soup, meat, stuffing and mixed greens.

Rosemary Very aromatic. Can be used fresh or dried. Season fish, stuffing, beef, lamb, poultry, onions, eggs, bread and potatoes. Great in dressings.

Saffron Orange-yellow in color, this spice flavors or colors foods. Use in soup, chicken, rice and breads.

Sage Use fresh or dried. The flowers are sometimes used in salads. May be used in tomato juice, fish, omelets, beef, poultry, stuffing, cheese spreads and breads.

Tarragon Leaves have a pungent, hot taste. Use to flavor sauces, salads, fish, poultry, tomatoes, eggs, green beans, carrots and dressings.

Thyme Sprinkle leaves on fish or poultry before broiling or baking. Throw a few sprigs directly on coals shortly before meat is finished grilling.

Baking Breads

Hints for Baking Breads

1. Kneading dough for 30 seconds after mixing improves the texture of baking powder biscuits.

2. Instead of shortening, use cooking or salad oil in waffles and hot cakes.

3. When bread is baking, a small dish of water in the oven will help keep the crust from hardening.

4. Dip a spoon in hot water to measure shortening, butter, etc., and the fat will slip out more easily.

5. Small amounts of leftover corn may be added to pancake batter for variety.

6. To make bread crumbs, use the fine cutter of a food grinder and tie a large paper bag over the spout in order to prevent flying crumbs.

7. When you are doing any sort of baking, you get better results if you remember to preheat your cookie sheet, muffin tins or cake pans.

Rules for Use of Leavening Agents

1. In simple flour mixtures, use 2 teaspoons baking powder to leaven 1 cup flour. Reduce this amount 1/2 teaspoon for each egg used.

2. To 1 teaspoon soda use 2 1/4 teaspoons cream of tartar, 2 cups freshly soured milk, or 1 cup molasses.

3. To substitute soda and an acid for baking powder, divide the amount of baking powder by 4. Take that as your measure and add acid according to rule 2.

Proportions of Baking Powder to Flour

biscuits	to 1 cup flour use 1 1/4 tsp. baking powder
cake with oil	to 1 cup flour use 1 tsp. baking powder
muffins	to 1 cup flour use 1 1/2 tsp. baking powder
popovers	to 1 cup flour use 1 1/4 tsp. baking powder
waffles	to 1 cup flour use 1 1/4 tsp. baking powder

Proportions of Liquid to Flour

drop batter	to 1 cup liquid use 2 to 2 1/2 cups flour
pour batter	to 1 cup liquid use 1 cup flour
soft dough	to 1 cup liquid use 3 to 3 1/2 cups flour
stiff dough	to 1 cup liquid use 4 cups flour

Time and Temperature Chart

Breads	Minutes	Temperature
biscuits	12 - 15	400° - 450°
cornbread	25 - 30	400° - 425°
gingerbread	40 - 50	350° - 370°
loaf	50 - 60	350° - 400°
nut bread	50 - 75	350°
popovers	30 - 40	425° - 450°
rolls	20 - 30	400° - 450°

Baking Desserts

Perfect Cookies

Cookie dough that is to be rolled is much easier to handle after it has been refrigerated for 10 to 30 minutes. This keeps the dough from sticking, even though it may be soft. If not done, the soft dough may require more flour and too much flour makes cookies hard and brittle. Place on a floured board only as much dough as can be easily managed.

Flour the rolling pin slightly and roll lightly to desired thickness. Cut shapes close together and add trimmings to dough that needs to be rolled. Place pans or sheets in upper third of oven. Watch cookies carefully while baking in order to avoid burned edges. When sprinkling sugar on cookies, try putting it into a salt shaker in order to save time.

Perfect Pies

1. Pie crust will be better and easier to make if all the ingredients are cool.

2. The lower crust should be placed in the pan so that it covers the surface smoothly. Air pockets beneath the surface will push the crust out of shape while baking.

3. Folding the top crust over the lower crust before crimping will keep juices in the pie.

4. In making custard pie, bake at a high temperature for about ten minutes to prevent a soggy crust. Then finish baking at a low temperature.

5. When making cream pie, sprinkle crust with powdered sugar in order to prevent it from becoming soggy.

Perfect Cakes

1. Fill cake pans two-thirds full and spread batter into corners and sides, leaving a slight hollow in the center.

2. Cake is done when it shrinks from the sides of the pan or if it springs back when touched lightly with the finger.

3. After removing a cake from the oven, place it on a rack for about five minutes. Then, the sides should be loosened and the cake turned out on a rack in order to finish cooling.

4. Do not frost cakes until thoroughly cool.

5. Icing will remain where you put it if you sprinkle cake with powdered sugar first.

Time and Temperature Chart

Dessert	Time	Temperature
butter cake, layer	20-40 min.	380° - 400°
butter cake, loaf	40-60 min.	360° - 400°
cake, angel	50-60 min.	300° - 360°
cake, fruit	3-4 hrs.	275° - 325°
cake, sponge	40-60 min.	300° - 350°
cookies, molasses	18-20 min.	350° - 375°
cookies, thin	10-12 min.	380° - 390°
cream puffs	45-60 min.	300° - 350°
meringue	40-60 min.	250° - 300°
pie crust	20-40 min.	400° - 500°

Vegetables & Fruits

Vegetable	Cooking Method	Time
artichokes	boiled	40 min.
	steamed	45-60 min.
asparagus tips	boiled	10-15 min.
beans, lima	boiled	20-40 min.
	steamed	60 min.
beans, string	boiled	15-35 min.
	steamed	60 min.
beets, old	boiled or steamed	1-2 hours
beets, young with skin	boiled	30 min.
	steamed	60 min.
	baked	70-90 min.
broccoli, flowerets	boiled	5-10 min.
broccoli, stems	boiled	20-30 min.
brussels sprouts	boiled	20-30 min.
cabbage, chopped	boiled	10-20 min.
	steamed	25 min.
carrots, cut across	boiled	8-10 min.
	steamed	40 min.
cauliflower, flowerets	boiled	8-10 min.
cauliflower, stem down	boiled	20-30 min.
corn, green, tender	boiled	5-10 min.
	steamed	15 min.
	baked	20 min.
corn on the cob	boiled	8-10 min.
	steamed	15 min.
eggplant, whole	boiled	30 min.
	steamed	40 min.
	baked	45 min.
parsnips	boiled	25-40 min.
	steamed	60 min.
	baked	60-75 min.
peas, green	boiled or steamed	5-15 min.
potatoes	boiled	20-40 min.
	steamed	60 min.
	baked	45-60 min.
pumpkin or squash	boiled	20-40 min.
	steamed	45 min.
	baked	60 min.
tomatoes	boiled	5-15 min.
turnips	boiled	25-40 min.

Drying Time Table

Fruit	Sugar or Honey	Cooking Time
apricots	1/4 c. for each cup of fruit	about 40 min.
figs	1 T. for each cup of fruit	about 30 min.
peaches	1/4 c. for each cup of fruit	about 45 min.
prunes	2 T. for each cup of fruit	about 45 min.

Vegetables & Fruits

Buying Fresh Vegetables

Artichokes: Look for compact, tightly closed heads with green, clean-looking leaves. Avoid those with leaves that are brown or separated.

Asparagus: Stalks should be tender and firm; tips should be close and compact. Choose the stalks with very little white; they are more tender. Use asparagus soon because it toughens rapidly.

Beans, Snap: Those with small seeds inside the pods are best. Avoid beans with dry-looking pods.

Broccoli, Brussels Sprouts and Cauliflower: Flower clusters on broccoli and cauliflower should be tight and close together. Brussels sprouts should be firm and compact. Smudgy, dirty spots may indicate pests or disease.

Cabbage and Head Lettuce: Choose heads that are heavy for their size. Avoid cabbage with worm holes and lettuce with discoloration or soft rot.

Cucumbers: Choose long, slender cucumbers for best quality. May be dark or medium green, but yellow ones are undesirable.

Mushrooms: Caps should be closed around the stems. Avoid black or brown gills.

Peas and Lima Beans: Select pods that are well-filled but not bulging. Avoid dried, spotted, yellow, or flabby pods.

Buying Fresh Fruits

Bananas: Skin should be free of bruises and black or brown spots. Purchase them green and allow them to ripen at home at room temperature.

Berries: Select plump, solid berries with good color. Avoid stained containers which indicate wet or leaky berries. Berries with clinging caps, such as blackberries and raspberries, may be unripe. Strawberries without caps may be overripe.

Melons: In cantaloupes, thick, close netting on the rind indicates best quality. Cantaloupes are ripe when the stem scar is smooth and the space between the netting is yellow or yellow-green. They are best when fully ripe with fruity odor.

Honeydews are ripe when rind has creamy to yellowish color and velvety texture. Immature honeydews are whitish-green.

Ripe watermelons have some yellow color on one side. If melons are white or pale green on one side, they are not ripe.

Oranges, Grapefruit and Lemons: Choose those heavy for their size. Smoother, thinner skins usually indicate more juice. Most skin markings do not affect quality. Oranges with a slight greenish tinge may be just as ripe as fully colored ones. Light or greenish-yellow lemons are more tart than deep yellow ones. Avoid citrus fruits showing withered, sunken or soft areas.

Napkin Folding

General Tips:

Use well-starched linen napkins if possible. For more complicated folds, 24-inch napkins work best. Practice the folds with newspapers. Children can help. Once they learn the folds, they will have fun!

Shield

Easy fold. Elegant with monogram in corner.

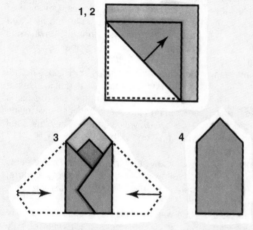

Instructions:

1. Fold into quarter size. If monogrammed, ornate corner should face down.
2. Turn up folded corner three-quarters.
3. Overlap right side and left side points.
4. Turn over; adjust sides so that they are even, single point in center.
5. Place point up or down on plate, or left of plate.

Rosette

Elegant on plate.

Instructions:

1. Fold left and right edges to center, leaving ½" opening along center.
2. Pleat firmly from top edge to bottom edge. Sharpen edges with hot iron.
3. Pinch center together. If necessary, use small piece of pipe cleaner to secure and top with single flower.
4. Spread out rosette.

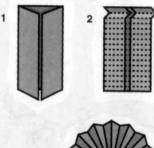

Napkin Folding

Candle

Easy to do; can be decorated.

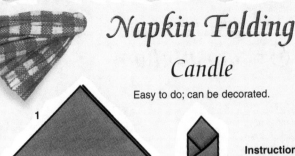

Instructions:
1. Fold into triangle, point at top.
2. Turn lower edge up 1".
3. Turn over, folded edge down.
4. Roll tightly from left to right.
5. Tuck in corner. Stand upright.

Fan

Pretty in napkin ring or on plate.

Instructions:
1. Fold top and bottom edges to center.
2. Fold top and bottom edges to center a second time.
3. Pleat firmly from the left edge. Sharpen edges with hot iron.
4. Spread out fan. Balance flat folds of each side on table. Well-starched napkins will hold shape.

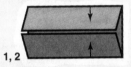

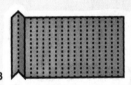

Lily

Effective and pretty on table.

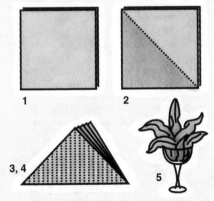

Instructions:
1. Fold napkin into quarters.
2. Fold into triangle, closed corner to open points.
3. Turn two points over to other side. (Two points are on either side of closed point.)
4. Pleat.
5. Place closed end in glass. Pull down two points on each side and shape.

Measurements & Substitutions

Measurements

a pinch	1/8 teaspoon or less
3 teaspoons	1 tablespoon
4 tablespoons	1/4 cup
8 tablespoons	1/2 cup
12 tablespoons	3/4 cup
16 tablespoons	1 cup
2 cups	1 pint
4 cups	1 quart
4 quarts	1 gallon
8 quarts	1 peck
4 pecks	1 bushel
16 ounces	1 pound
32 ounces	1 quart
1 ounce liquid	2 tablespoons
8 ounces liquid	1 cup

**Use standard measuring spoons and cups.
All measurements are level.**

Substitutions

Ingredient	Quantity	Substitute
baking powder	1 teaspoon	1/4 tsp. baking soda plus 1/2 tsp. cream of tartar
catsup or chili sauce	1 cup	1 c. tomato sauce plus 1/2 c. sugar and 2 T. vinegar (for use in cooking)
chocolate	1 square (1 oz.)	3 or 4 T. cocoa plus 1 T. butter
cornstarch	1 tablespoon	2 T. flour or 2 tsp. quick-cooking tapioca
cracker crumbs	3/4 cup	1 c. bread crumbs
dates	1 lb.	1 1/2 c. dates, pitted and cut
dry mustard	1 teaspoon	1 T. prepared mustard
flour, self-rising	1 cup	1 c. all-purpose flour, 1/2 tsp. salt, and 1 tsp. baking powder
herbs, fresh	1 tablespoon	1 tsp. dried herbs
milk, sour	1 cup	1 T. lemon juice or vinegar plus sweet milk to make 1 c. (let stand 5 minutes)
whole	1 cup	1/2 c. evaporated milk plus 1/2 c. water
min. marshmallows	10	1 lg. marshmallow
onion, fresh	1 small	1 T. instant minced onion, rehydrated
sugar, brown	1/2 cup	2 T. molasses in 1/2 c. granulated sugar
powdered	1 cup	1 c. granulated sugar plus 1 tsp. cornstarch
tomato juice	1 cup	1/2 c. tomato sauce plus 1/2 c. water

**When substituting cocoa for chocolate in cakes, the amount of flour must
be reduced. Brown and white sugars usually can be interchanged.**

Equivalency Chart

Food	Quantity	Yield
apple	1 medium	1 cup
banana, mashed	1 medium	1/3 cup
bread	1 1/2 slices	1 cup soft crumbs
bread	1 slice	1/4 cup fine, dry crumbs
butter	1 stick or 1/4 pound	1/2 cup
cheese, American, cubed	1 pound	2 2/3 cups
American, grated	1 pound	5 cups
cream cheese	3-ounce package	6 2/3 tablespoons
chocolate, bitter	1 square	1 ounce
cocoa	1 pound	4 cups
coconut	1 1/2 pound package	2 2/3 cups
coffee, ground	1 pound	5 cups
cornmeal	1 pound	3 cups
cornstarch	1 pound	3 cups
crackers, graham	14 squares	1 cup fine crumbs
saltine	28 crackers	1 cup fine crumbs
egg	4-5 whole	1 cup
whites	8-10	1 cup
yolks	10-12	1 cup
evaporated milk	1 cup	3 cups whipped
flour, cake, sifted	1 pound	4 1/2 cups
rye	1 pound	5 cups
white, sifted	1 pound	4 cups
white, unsifted	1 pound	3 3/4 cups
gelatin, flavored	3 1/4 ounces	1/2 cup
unflavored	1/4 ounce	1 tablespoon
lemon	1 medium	3 tablespoon juice
marshmallows	16	1/4 pound
noodles, cooked	8-ounce package	7 cups
uncooked	4 ounces (1 1/2 cups)	2-3 cups cooked
macaroni, cooked	8-ounce package	6 cups
macaroni, uncooked	4 ounces (1 1/4 cups)	2 1/4 cups cooked
spaghetti, uncooked	7 ounces	4 cups cooked
nuts, chopped	1/4 pound	1 cup
almonds	1 pound	3 1/2 cups
walnuts, broken	1 pound	3 cups
walnuts, unshelled	1 pound	1 1/2 to 1 3/4 cups
onion	1 medium	1/2 cup
orange	3-4 medium	1 cup juice
raisins	1 pound	3 1/2 cups
rice, brown	1 cup	4 cups cooked
converted	1 cup	3 1/2 cups cooked
regular	1 cup	3 cups cooked
wild	1 cup	4 cups cooked
sugar, brown	1 pound	2 1/2 cups
powdered	1 pound	3 1/2 cups
white	1 pound	2 cups
vanilla wafers	22	1 cup fine crumbs
zwieback, crumbled	4	1 cups

Food Quantities
For Large Servings

	25 Servings	50 Servings	100 Servings
Beverages:			
coffee	½ pound and 1 ½ gallons water	1 pound and 3 gallons water	2 pounds and 6 gallons water
lemonade	10-15 lemons and 1 ½ gallons water	20-30 lemons and 3 gallons water	40-60 lemons and 6 gallons water
tea	¹/₁₂ pound and 1 ½ gallons water	⅙ pound and 3 gallons water	⅓ pound and 6 gallons water
Desserts:			
layered cake	1 12" cake	3 10" cakes	6 10" cakes
sheet cake	1 10" x 12" cake	1 12" x 20" cake	2 12" x 20" cakes
watermelon	37 ½ pounds	75 pounds	150 pounds
whipping cream	¾ pint	1 ½ to 2 pints	3-4 pints
Ice cream:			
brick	3 ¼ quarts	6 ½ quarts	13 quarts
bulk	2 ¼ quarts	4 ½ quarts or 1 ¼ gallons	9 quarts or 2 ½ gallons
Meat, poultry or fish:			
fish	13 pounds	25 pounds	50 pounds
fish, fillets or steak	7 ½ pounds	15 pounds	30 pounds
hamburger	9 pounds	18 pounds	35 pounds
turkey or chicken	13 pounds	25 to 35 pounds	50 to 75 pounds
wieners (beef)	6 ½ pounds	13 pounds	25 pounds
Salads, casseroles:			
baked beans	¾ gallon	1 ¼ gallons	2 ½ gallons
jello salad	¾ gallon	1 ¼ gallons	2 ½ gallons
potato salad	4 ¼ quarts	2 ¼ gallons	4 ½ gallons
scalloped potatoes	4 ½ quarts or 1 12" x 20" pan	9 quarts or 2 ¼ gallons	18 quarts 4 ½ gallons
spaghetti	1 ¼ gallons	2 ½ gallons	5 gallons
Sandwiches:			
bread	50 slices or 3 1-pound loaves	100 slices or 6 1-pound loaves	200 slices or 12 1-pound loaves
butter	½ pound	1 pound	2 pounds
lettuce	1 ½ heads	3 heads	6 heads
mayonnaise	1 cup	2 cups	4 cups
mixed filling			
meat, eggs, fish	1 ½ quarts	3 quarts	6 quarts
jam, jelly	1 quart	2 quarts	4 quarts

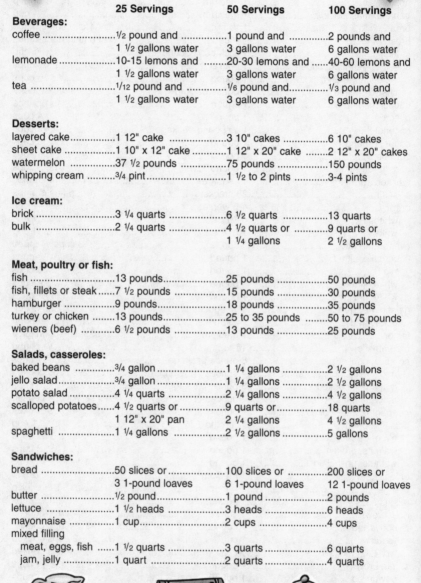

Microwave Hints

1. Place an open box of hardened brown sugar in the microwave oven with 1 cup hot water. Microwave on high for 1 1/2 to 2 minutes for 1/2 pound or 2 to 3 minutes for 1 pound.

2. Soften hard ice cream by microwaving at 30% power. One pint will take 15 to 30 seconds; one quart, 30-45 seconds; and one-half gallon, 45-60 seconds.

3. To melt chocolate, place 1/2 pound in glass bowl or measuring cup. Melt uncovered at 50% power for 3-4 minutes; stir after 2 minutes.

4. Soften one 8-ounce package of cream cheese by microwaving at 30% power for 2 to 2 1/2 minutes. One 3-ounce package of cream cheese will soften in 1 1/2 to 2 minutes.

5. A 4 1/2 ounce carton of whipped topping will thaw in 1 minute on the defrost setting. Whipped topping should be slightly firm in the center, but it will blend well when stirred. Do not over thaw!

6. Soften jello that has set up too hard - perhaps you were to chill it until slightly thickened and forgot it. Heat on a low power setting for a very short time.

7. Heat hot packs. A wet fingertip towel will take about 25 seconds. It depends on the temperature of the water used to wet the towel.

8. To scald milk, cook 1 cup for 2 to 2 1/2 minutes, stirring once each minute.

9. To make dry bread crumbs, cut 6 slices of bread into 1/2-inch cubes. Microwave in 3-quart casserole 6-7 minutes, or until dry, stirring after 3 minutes. Crush in blender.

10. Refresh stale potato chips, crackers or other snacks of such type by putting a plateful in the microwave for 30-45 seconds. Let stand for 1 minute to crisp. Cereals can also be crisped.

11. Nuts will be easier to shell if you place 2 cups of nuts in a 1-quart casserole with 1 cup of water. Cook for 4 to 5 minutes and the nutmeats will slip out whole after cracking the shell.

12. Stamp collectors can place a few drops of water on a stamp to remove it from an envelope. Heat in the microwave for 20 seconds, and the stamp will come off.

13. Using a round dish instead of a square one eliminates overcooked corners in baking cakes.

14. Sprinkle a layer of medium, finely chopped walnuts evenly onto the bottom and side of a ring pan or bundt cake pan to enhances the looks and eating quality. Pour in batter and microwave as recipe directs.

15. Do not salt foods on the surface as it causes dehydration and toughens food. Salt after you remove from the oven unless the recipe calls for using salt in the mixture.

16. Heat left-over custard and use it as frosting for a cake.

17. Melt marshmallow creme. Half of a 7-ounce jar will melt in 35-40 seconds on high. Stir to blend.

18. To toast coconut, spread 1/2 cup coconut in a pie plate and cook for 3-4 minutes, stirring every 30 seconds after 2 minutes. Watch closely, as it quickly browns.

19. To melt crystallized honey, heat uncovered jar on high for 30-45 seconds. If jar is large, repeat.

20. One stick of butter or margarine will soften in 1 minute when microwaved at 20% power.

Calorie Counter

Beverages

apple juice, 6 oz.	90
coffee (black)	0
cola type, 12 oz.	115
cranberry juice, 6 oz.	115
ginger ale, 12 oz.	115
grape juice, (prepared from frozen concentrate), 6 oz.	142
lemonade, (prepared from frozen concentrate), 6 oz.	85
milk, protein fortified, 1 c.	105
skim, 1 c.	90
whole, 1 c.	160
orange juice, 6 oz.	85
pineapple juice, unsweetened, 6 oz.	95
root beer, 12 oz.	150
tonic (quinine water) 12 oz.	132

Breads

cornbread, 1 sm. square	130
dumplings, 1 med.	70
French toast, 1 slice	135
melba toast, 1 slice	25
muffins, blueberry, 1 muffin	110
bran, 1 muffin	106
corn, 1 muffin	125
English, 1 muffin	280
pancakes, 1 (4-in.)	60
pumpernickel, 1 slice	75
rye, 1 slice	60
waffle, 1	216
white, 1 slice	60-70
whole wheat, 1 slice	55-65

Cereals

cornflakes, 1 c.	105
cream of wheat, 1 c.	120
oatmeal, 1 c.	148
rice flakes, 1 c.	105
shredded wheat, 1 biscuit	100
sugar krisps, 3/4 c.	110

Crackers

graham, 1 cracker	15-30
rye crisp, 1 cracker	35
saltine, 1 cracker	17-20
wheat thins, 1 cracker	9

Dairy Products

butter or margarine, 1 T.	100
cheese, American, 1 oz.	100
camembert, 1 oz.	85
cheddar, 1 oz.	115
cottage cheese, 1 oz.	30
mozzarella, 1 oz.	90
parmesan, 1 oz.	130
ricotta, 1 oz.	50
roquefort, 1 oz.	105
Swiss, 1 oz.	105
cream, light, 1 T.	30
heavy, 1 T.	55
sour, 1 T.	45
hot chocolate, with milk, 1 c.	277
milk chocolate, 1 oz.	145-155
yogurt	
made w/ whole milk, 1 c.	150-165
made w/ skimmed milk, 1 c.	125

Eggs

fried, 1 lg.	100
poached or boiled, 1 lg.	75-80
scrambled or in omelet, 1 lg.	110-130

Fish and Seafood

bass, 4 oz.	105
salmon, broiled or baked, 3 oz.	155
sardines, canned in oil, 3 oz.	170
trout, fried, 3 1/2 oz.	220
tuna, in oil, 3 oz.	170
in water, 3 oz.	110

Calorie Counter

Fruits

apple, 1 med.	80-100
applesauce, sweetened, 1/2 c.	90-115
unsweetened, 1/2 c.	50
banana, 1 med.	85
blueberries, 1/2 c.	45
cantaloupe, 1/2 c.	24
cherries (pitted), raw, 1/2 c.	40
grapefruit, 1/2 med.	55
grapes, 1/2 c.	35-55
honeydew, 1/2 c.	55
mango, 1 med.	90
orange, 1 med.	65-75
peach, 1 med.	35
pear, 1 med.	60-100
pineapple, fresh, 1/2 c.	40
canned in syrup, 1/2 c.	95
plum, 1 med.	30
strawberries, fresh, 1/2 c.	30
frozen and sweetened, 1/2 c.	120-140
tangerine, 1 lg.	39
watermelon, 1/2 c.	42

Meat and Poultry

beef, ground (lean), 3 oz.	185
roast, 3 oz.	185
chicken, broiled, 3 oz.	115
lamb chop (lean), 3 oz.	175-200
steak, sirloin, 3 oz.	175
tenderloin, 3 oz.	174
top round, 3 oz.	162
turkey, dark meat, 3 oz.	175
white meat, 3 oz.	150
veal, cutlet, 3 oz.	156
roast, 3 oz.	76

Nuts

almonds, 2 T.	105
cashews, 2 T.	100
peanuts, 2 T.	105
peanut butter, 1 T.	95
pecans, 2 T.	95
pistachios, 2 T.	92
walnuts, 2 T.	80

Pasta

macaroni or spaghetti, cooked, 3/4 c.	115

Salad Dressings

blue cheese, 1 T.	70
French, 1 T.	65
Italian, 1 T.	80
mayonnaise, 1 T.	100
olive oil, 1 T.	124
Russian, 1 T.	70
salad oil, 1 T.	120

Soups

bean, 1 c.	130-180
beef noodle, 1 c.	70
bouillon and consomme, 1 c.	30
chicken noodle, 1 c.	65
chicken with rice, 1 c.	50
minestrone, 1 c.	80-150
split pea, 1 c.	145-170
tomato with milk, 1 c.	170
vegetable, 1 c.	80-100

Vegetables

asparagus, 1 c.	35
broccoli, cooked, 1/2 c.	25
cabbage, cooked, 1/2 c.	15-20
carrots, cooked, 1/2 c.	25-30
cauliflower, 1/2 c.	10-15
corn (kernels), 1/2 c.	70
green beans, 1 c.	30
lettuce, shredded, 1/2 c.	5
mushrooms, canned, 1/2 c.	20
onions, cooked, 1/2 c.	30
peas, cooked, 1/2 c.	60
potato, baked, 1 med.	90
chips, 8-10	100
mashed, w/milk & butter, 1 c.	200-300
spinach, 1 c.	40
tomato, raw, 1 med.	25
cooked, 1/2 c.	30

Cooking Terms

Au gratin: Topped with crumbs and/or cheese and browned in oven or under broiler.

Au jus: Served in its own juices.

Baste: To moisten foods during cooking with pan drippings or special sauce in order to add flavor and prevent drying.

Bisque: A thick cream soup.

Blanch: To immerse in rapidly boiling water and allow to cook slightly.

Cream: To soften a fat, especially butter, by beating it at room temperature. Butter and sugar are often creamed together, making a smooth, soft paste.

Crimp: To seal the edges of a two-crust pie either by pinching them at intervals with the fingers or by pressing them together with the tines of a fork.

Crudites: An assortment of raw vegetables (i.e. carrots, broccoli, celery, mushrooms) that is served as an hors d'oeuvre, often accompanied by a dip.

Degrease: To remove fat from the surface of stews, soups, or stock. Usually cooled in the refrigerator so that fat hardens and is easily removed.

Dredge: To coat lightly with flour, cornmeal, etc.

Entree: The main course.

Fold: To incorporate a delicate substance, such as whipped cream or beaten egg whites, into another substance without releasing air bubbles. A spatula is used to gently bring part of the mixture from the bottom of the bowl to the top. The process is repeated, while slowly rotating the bowl, until the ingredients are thoroughly blended.

Glaze: To cover with a glossy coating, such as a melted and somewhat diluted jelly for fruit desserts.

Julienne: To cut vegetables, fruits, or cheeses into match-shaped slivers.

Marinate: To allow food to stand in a liquid in order to tenderize or to add flavor.

Meuniére: Dredged with flour and sautéed in butter.

Mince: To chop food into very small pieces.

Parboil: To boil until partially cooked; to blanch. Usually final cooking in a seasoned sauce follows this procedure.

Pare: To remove the outermost skin of a fruit or vegetable.

Poach: To cook gently in hot liquid kept just below the boiling point.

Purée: To mash foods by hand by rubbing through a sieve or food mill, or by whirling in a blender or food processor until perfectly smooth.

Refresh: To run cold water over food that has been parboiled in order to stop the cooking process quickly.

Sauté: To cook and/or brown food in a small quantity of hot shortening.

Scald: To heat to just below the boiling point, when tiny bubbles appear at the edge of the saucepan.

Simmer: To cook in liquid just below the boiling point. The surface of the liquid should be barely moving, broken from time to time by slowly rising bubbles.

Steep: To let food stand in hot liquid in order to extract or to enhance flavor, like tea in hot water or poached fruit in sugar syrup.

Toss: To combine ingredients with a repeated lifting motion.

Whip: To beat rapidly in order to incorporate air and produce expansion, as in heavy cream or egg whites.

Morris Press Cookbooks has all the right ingredients to make a really great cookbook. Your group can raise $500–$50,000 or create a cookbook as a lasting keepsake, preserving favorite family recipes.

3 ways to order our **FREE** Cookbook Kit:
- Call us at **800-445-6621, ext. CB**.
- Visit our web site at **www.morriscookbooks.com**.
- Complete and mail the **postage-paid reply card** below.